UNDERSTANDING SHARON OLDS

UNDERSTANDING CONTEMPORARY AMERICAN LITERATURE

Matthew J. Bruccoli, Founding Editor

Linda Wagner-Martin, Series Editor

Volumes on

Edward Albee | Sherman Alexie | Nelson Algren | Paul Auster
Nicholson Baker | John Barth | Donald Barthelme | The Beats
Thomas Berger | The Black Mountain Poets | Robert Bly | T. C. Boyle
Truman Capote | Raymond Carver | Michael Chabon | Fred Chappell
Chicano Literature | Contemporary American Drama
Contemporary American Horror Fiction
Contemporary American Literary Theory
Contemporary American Science Fiction, 1926–1970
Contemporary American Science Fiction, 1970–2000
Contemporary Chicana Literature | Pat Conroy | Robert Coover | Don DeLillo
Philip K. Dick | James Dickey | E. L. Doctorow | Rita Dove | Dave Eggers
Louise Erdrich | John Gardner | George Garrett | Tim Gautreaux | William Gibson
John Hawkes | Joseph Heller | Lillian Hellman | Beth Henley | James Leo Herlihy
David Henry Hwang | John Irving | Randall Jarrell | Gish Jen | Charles Johnson
Diane Johnson | Edward P. Jones | Adrienne Kennedy | William Kennedy | Jack Kerouac
Jamaica Kincaid | Etheridge Knight | Tony Kushner | Ursula K. Le Guin
Jonathan Lethem | Denise Levertov | Bernard Malamud | David Mamet
Bobbie Ann Mason | Colum McCann | Cormac McCarthy | Jill McCorkle
Carson McCullers | W. S. Merwin | Arthur Miller | Stephen Millhauser | Lorrie Moore
Toni Morrison's Fiction | Vladimir Nabokov | Gloria Naylor | Joyce Carol Oates
Tim O'Brien | Flannery O'Connor | Sharon Olds | Cynthia Ozick | Chuck Palahniuk
Suzan-Lori Parks | Walker Percy | Katherine Anne Porter | Richard Powers
Reynolds Price | Annie Proulx | Thomas Pynchon | Ron Rash | Adrienne Rich
Theodore Roethke | Philip Roth | Richard Russo | May Sarton | Hubert Selby, Jr.
Mary Lee Settle | Sam Shepard | Neil Simon | Isaac Bashevis Singer | Jane Smiley
Gary Snyder | Susan Sontag | William Stafford | Robert Stone | Anne Tyler
Gerald Vizenor | Kurt Vonnegut | David Foster Wallace | Robert Penn Warren
James Welch | Eudora Welty | Edmund White | Colson Whitehead
Tennessee Williams | August Wilson | Charles Wright

UNDERSTANDING SHAROn OLDS

Russell Brickey

The University of South Carolina Press

Published by the University of South Carolina Press
Columbia, South Carolina 29208

www.sc.edu/uscpress

Manufactured in the United States of America

26 25 24 23 22 21 20 19 18 17
10 9 8 7 6 5 4 3 2 1

Library of Congress Cataloging-in-Publication Data
can be found at http://catalog.loc.gov/.

ISBN 978-1-61117-711-4 (cloth)
ISBN 978-1-61117-712-1 (ebook)

This book was printed on recycled paper with
30 percent postconsumer waste content.

CONTENTS

SERIES EDITOR'S PREFACE

The Understanding Contemporary American Literature series was founded by the estimable Matthew J. Bruccoli (1931–2008), who envisioned these volumes as guides or companions for students as well as good nonacademic readers, a legacy that will continue as new volumes are developed to fill in gaps among the nearly one hundred series volumes published to date and to embrace a host of new writers only now making their marks on our literature.

As Professor Bruccoli explained in his preface to the volumes he edited, because much influential contemporary literature makes special demands, "the word *understanding* in the titles was chosen deliberately. Many willing readers lack an adequate understanding of how contemporary literature works; that is, of what the author is attempting to express and the means by which it is conveyed." Aimed at fostering this understanding of good literature and good writers, the criticism and analysis in the series provide instruction in how to read certain contemporary writers—explicating their material, language, structures, themes, and perspectives—and facilitate a more profitable experience of the works under discussion.

In the twenty-first century Professor Bruccoli's prescience gives us an avenue to publish expert critiques of significant contemporary American writing. The series continues to map the literary landscape and to provide both instruction and enjoyment. Future volumes will seek to introduce new voices alongside canonized favorites, to chronicle the changing literature of our times, and to remain, as Professor Bruccoli conceived, contemporary in the best sense of the word.

Linda Wagner-Martin, Series Editor

ACKNOWLEDGMENTS

Quotations from the following sources are reprinted by permission of the University of Pittsburgh Press:

"Satan Says," "Love Fossil," "Tricks," "Late," "The Housewives Watching Morning TV," "Republican Living Rooms" from *Satan Says* by Sharon Olds, copyright © 1980 by permission of The University of Pittsburgh Press.

Quotations from the following sources are reprinted by permission of Knopf Doubleday Publishing Group, a division of Penguin Random House LLC:

"Sex without Love," "The Victims," "The Guild," "The Death of Marilyn Monroe," "New Mother," "The End," "The Moment," "Photograph of the Girl," "The Connoisseuse of Slugs," "The Pact," "Ideographs," "The Issues," "Nevsky Prospekt," "Absent One," "Possessed," "The Departure," "Burn Center," "The Ideal Father," "Fate," "My Father Snoring," "My Father's Breasts," "The Takers," "Poem to My First Lover," "The Line," "Poem to My Husband from My Father's Daughter," "Ecstasy," "Exclusive," "Six-Year-Old Boy," "Eggs," "For My Daughter," "The Sign of Saturn," and "Race Riot, Tulsa, 1921" from *The Dead and the Living* by Sharon Olds, copyright © 1987 by Sharon Olds. Used by permission of Alfred A. Knopf, an imprint of the Knopf Doubleday Publishing Group, a division of Penguin Random House LLC. All rights reserved.

"I Go Back to May 1937," "On the Subway," "Summer Solstice, New York City," "The Abandoned Newborn," "The Girl," "After 37 Years My Mother Apologizes for My Childhood," "Why My Mother Made Me," "Saturn," "When," "The Solution," "In the Cell," "The Twin," and "The Meal" from *The Gold Cell* by Sharon Olds, copyright © 1987 by Sharon Olds. Used by permission of Alfred A. Knopf, an imprint of the Knopf Doubleday Publishing Group, a division of Penguin Random House LLC. All rights reserved.

"The Glass," "Nullipara," "His Terror," "His Stillness," "The Waiting," "Wonder," "My Father Speaks to Me from the Dead," "The Pulling," "Death and Morality," "The Lumens," "The Want," "The Present Moment," "Beyond Harm," "My Father's Eyes," "The Underlife," "The Ferryer," "When the Dead Ask My

Father about Me," and "Waste Sonata" from *The Father* by Sharon Olds, copyright © 1992 by Sharon Olds. Used by permission of Alfred A. Knopf, an imprint of the Knopf Doubleday Publishing Group, a division of Penguin Random House LLC. All rights reserved.

"Visiting My Mother's College," "Japanese-American Farmhouse, California, 1942," "First Birth," "Her First Week," "Celibacy at Twenty," "Socks," "Bathing the New Born," "Adolescence," "May 1968," "History of Medicine," "Good Will," "My Parents' Wedding Night, 1937," "The Swimming Race," "First," "Early Images of Heaven," "The Source," "Making Love," "I Love It When," "Milk-Bubble Ruins," "Twelve Years Old," "Lament," and "Solo" from *The Wellspring: Poems* by Sharon Olds, copyright © 1996 by Sharon Olds. Used by permission of Alfred A. Knopf, an imprint of the Knopf Doubleday Publishing Group, a division of Penguin Random House LLC. All rights reserved.

"Once," "Take the I Out," "Electricity Saviour," "My Father's Diary," "Animal Music," "Aspic and Buttermilk," "Poem to the Reader," "The Bed," "The Try-Outs," "By Fire," and "For and against Knowledge" from *Blood, Tin, Straw: Poems* by Sharon Olds, copyright © 1999 by Sharon Olds. Used by permission of Alfred A. Knopf, an imprint of the Knopf Doubleday Publishing Group, a division of Penguin Random House LLC. All rights reserved.

"The Learner," "Sunday Night," "His Costume," "Directly," "The Older," "Fish Oil," "Mother," and "A Time of Passion" from *The Unswept Room* by Sharon Olds, copyright © 2002 by Sharon Olds. Used by permission of Alfred A. Knopf, an imprint of the Knopf Doubleday Publishing Group, a division of Penguin Random House LLC. All rights reserved.

"Diagnosis," "Satin Maroon," "1. Woman with the Lettuce," "2. Legless Fighter Pilot," "3. What Could Happen," "6. The Signal," "7. The Leader," "12. The Body," "The Cannery, 1942–1945," "At Night," "Freezer," "The Couldn't," "Paterfamilias," "Royal Beauty Bright," "The Riser," "Pansy Coda," "The Dead," "Good Measure," "2. The Music," "3. The Ecstatic," "4. Two Late Dialogues," "5. Warily, Sportsman!," "6. Little End Ode," "7. Something Is Happening," "8. Cassiopeia," "Still Life," "One Secret Thing," and "To See My Mother" from *One Secret Thing* by Sharon Olds, copyright © 2008 by Sharon Olds. Used by permission of Alfred A. Knopf, an imprint of the Knopf Doubleday Publishing Group, a division of Penguin Random House LLC. All rights reserved.

"Pain I Did Not," "The Healers," "While He Told Me," "Unspeakable," "The Flurry," "Stag's Leap," "Not Going to Him," "Once in a While I Gave Up," "French Bra," "Not Quite Enough," "Discandied," "Bruise Ghazal," "On Reading a Newspaper for the First Time as an Adult," "Slowly He Starts," "Red Sea,"

"Poem of Thanks," "Left-Wife Bop," "Years Later," "September 2001, New York City," and "What Left?" from *Stag's Leap: Poems* by Sharon Olds, copyright © 2012 by Sharon Olds. Used by permission of Alfred A. Knopf, an imprint of the Knopf Doubleday Publishing Group, a division of Penguin Random House LLC. All rights reserved.

ABBREVIATIONS FOR BOOKS BY SHARON OLDS

Blood, Tin, Straw (BTS)
The Dead and the Living (TDATL)
The Father (TF)
The Gold Cell (TGC)
One Secret Thing (OST)
Satan Says (SS)
Stag's Leap (SL)
The Unswept Room (TUR)
The Wellspring (TW)

CHAPTER 1

Understanding Sharon Olds

Much of what is publicly known about Sharon Olds the person comes directly from her poetry. She has steadfastly refused to discuss her personal life in interviews, an ironic stance considering that her poetry revolves around personal experience, often in intimate detail, and the lives of her family members, living and dead. Even the polite fiction that Olds's recurring narrator is not the poet herself collapses upon close examination: correspondences between her family members and her cast of characters are simply too close to be coincidence. Appropriately, perhaps, Olds prefers the term "personal" poet, as opposed to the more commonly applied "confessional" poet. In this regard she joins forces with the majority of those poets deemed confessional, virtually none of whom approved of the term foisted on them by critics and readers. Nonetheless Olds embodies the characteristics of what has come to be known, rightly or wrongly, as the confessional mode. Her verse is generally considered more accessible than those of her ostensible forebears—Robert Lowell, John Berryman, W. D. Snodgrass, Sylvia Plath, Anne Sexton, Adrienne Rich, and, particularly, Muriel Rukeyser—although the poetic lineage can be seen in Olds's themes of family cruelty and expansive imagery. Of particular note is the fact that Olds continues the confessional practice of dramatizing violent geopolitical conflicts through analogues to family dysfunction, and the same dynamics of cruelty and self-interest one sees in the microcosm of the family can be seen in the macrocosm of the dictator, the corrupt politician, or the specter of war. This is an underappreciated aspect of the confessional mode that Olds's poetry expands to its fullest, marking her as a true poet of the global age.

Born in San Francisco in 1942 to an iron salesman father and a music teacher mother, Olds describes her childhood self as "literal-minded and visually oriented,"[1] traits that later informed the creation of her poetry. As evidence of these propensities, at age two, when she was shown a book of World War II ration stamps and told that these were the family's source of food, Olds promptly retreated to a corner of the room and ate them. Other childhood memories provided fodder for her adult career as poet. The family lived near a school for the blind, for example, and young Olds sang with these students in an Episcopal choir. This experience inspired the poem "The Indispensability of the Eyes" (*SS* 8), which takes as its theme the vulnerability of blindness, which in turn equates to the vulnerability of women in general. These themes of womankind striving, vulnerable, but singing in the world are important to Olds's overall affirmation of renewal springing from physical and emotional danger.

As a young girl, Olds also had a propensity toward the romantic expressivity associated with the poetic temperament. "In the summer I went to Girl Scout camp," she recalls. "On special campfire nights, I would stand behind a Ponderosa pine and recite, in a loud quavery voice, homemade verses that began, 'I am the spirit of the tree.' I swam underwater as much as possible, and when no one was around I sometimes felt like a natural part of the earth."[2] Childhood was not a happy time, however. Olds has famously quipped that she grew up in a "hellfire Calvinist" family, enduring the cruelty of her grandfather, the emotional distance of her father, and the emotional instability of the mother—aspects of her life that can be gleaned from incidents described in the poetry. At age fifteen she attended a boarding school outside Boston, where the New England landscape and seasons enchanted her, and traveled to New York City, which Olds later described as "a mountain range made by people."

As an undergraduate at Stanford University, Olds studied the languages from which Western literature springs: French, Italian, German, Greek, and Middle English. After graduating with a bachelor's in languages from Stanford with distinction in 1964, she continued her studies at Columbia University, earning a Ph.D. in American literature in 1972; she wrote her dissertation on the prosody of Ralph Waldo Emerson. She also read contemporary poets Hugh Seidman, George Oppen, Clayton Eshleman, and Gary Snyder. Manhattan lived up to her expectations and has been Olds's home ever since.

It was also during this time that Olds made the decision to dedicate her life to poetry. Standing on the steps of the Columbia University library, she vowed to turn away from the poetry of the past and write in her own style, with her own voice, no matter how well or ill such poetry fared. Her first child was born during this time—a period in the United States fraught with cultural upheaval—and Olds divided her own energies between creativity and motherhood, what she describes as the study of "love, nourishment, healing and pleasure." Now a mother, she refused to put herself in harm's way by attending potentially dangerous antiwar protests and likewise avoided the hedonistic sexual politics of the time. Nevertheless the turbulent zeitgeist became a subject of her poetry. For a number of years she juggled writing with teaching at Sarah Lawrence College, the Theodor Herzl Institute, Brandeis University, and New York University. She also ran poetry workshops for the physically handicapped at Coler-Goldwater Hospital in New York City and worked with PEN Freedom-to-Write, Amnesty International, and Helsinki Watch. When she received the Lila Wallace–Reader's Digest Award in 1993, she used part of the money to benefit the Coler-Goldwater workshops. In recognition of her achievements, Olds served as New York's state poet laureate from 1998 to 2000.

In 2005 Olds garnered national attention after receiving an invitation from First Lady Laura Bush to attend the National Book Festival held in Washington, D.C., including a dinner at the Library of Congress and breakfast the next morning at the White House. Olds responded by publishing an open letter in the *Nation* on October 10 declining the offer, citing her objection to the Iraq War. Olds wrote, "So many Americans who had felt pride in our country now feel anguish and shame, for the current regime of blood, wounds and fire. I thought of the clean linens at your table, the shining knives and the flames of the candles, and I could not stomach it." Olds's poetry reflects this concern with empathy and humanity, as well as a polemical approach to politics, particularly war, and abuses of power.

Olds's first book of poetry, *Satan Says* (1980), published when the poet was thirty-seven, won the inaugural San Francisco Poetry Center Award. In some ways her most energetic book, *Satan Says* establishes many of Olds's overarching themes (patriarchal abuse, women's solidarity, sexuality, family dysfunction, and implicit arguments for empathy). The volume garnered mostly positive reviews, although some reviewers found the poetry hampered by the poet's inexperience. Her second collection, *The Dead and the Living* (1984), won two prestigious awards, the Lamont Poetry Prize and the National Book Critics Circle award; the collection has sold more than fifty thousand copies, making Olds one of the most widely read living poets. Her other books include *The Gold Cell* (1987); *The Father* (1992), about her father's death from cancer; *The Wellspring* (1995); *Blood, Tin, Straw* (1999); *The Unswept Room* (2002); and *One Secret Thing* (2008), about her mother's death from a stroke. However, while Olds's professional and publishing life established her as a leading poet and teacher, her personal life took a devastating turn in the late 1990s (she is reticent about specifics), when her husband, a doctor, left her for a colleague, sundering a marriage of more than thirty years. She wrote about the experience in private but held back publication of the poems for the sake of her family until 2013, when *Stag's Leap* was published and won both the

T. S. Eliot Prize and the Pulitzer Prize. Olds has been included in more than one hundred anthologies, and Web pages dedicated to her poetry proliferate, as do reviews of her works. Serious scholarly critique of her poetry is only now coming into vogue, suggesting that this most outspoken yet plainspoken writer is finally receiving much needed scholarly attention.

Olds remarried, to an environmentalist, and splits her time between New Hampshire and New York, where she still teaches at New York University. Her audience continues to grow, as does the number of her detractors, and her influence is increasingly apparent. She also continues to publish prolifically, making an overview of her work a daunting task that, of necessity, will here be incomplete.

Overview

First and foremost Olds is a memory poet. She harkens back to childhood, adolescence, and motherhood for the majority of her subject matter. Memories of her time as a young mother, most often when her children were infants or grade-school age, are tender but pointed reminders of the dangerous world outside the family. Recollections of her own childhood, on the other hand, are largely resentful dramatizations of alcoholism and the patriarchy—first-hand encounters with the dangerous world inside the family. The overall emotional thrust of her poems, those about her parents in particular, is predicated upon the ultimate effect these memories have on the adult speaker. These effects must often be inferred from the poems themselves. For instance part of what is so disturbing and fascinating about Olds's father character is the terrible loss of innocence; instead of childlike devotion, in "Love Fossil" (*SS* 5) the poet depicts a father figure wallowing in his own slow, stupid, self-centered impulses, apparently unaware of what the future holds or, if aware, unwilling to change. Similarly the mother is a demonic witch who destroys generations with her black magic in "Tricks" (*SS* 14). These two are stock characters in the cast of Olds's extended family drama; likewise her children, a son and daughter, and husband make their entrances and exits, as well as her sister, brother, and grandfather. The actors are almost never referred to by name in the poetry; Olds identifies her characters based on their family associations.

Olds's recurring first-person narrator, whose voice and memories form the core of her nine collections to date, is designated hereafter as "the daughter." The world is portrayed through the daughter's focalizing lens, replete with exaggerations and unapologetic biases. Her (fictional) autobiography undergirds the poetry in which both parents—their individual neuroses, their alcoholism, their abuses, their self-destructive tendencies—are the driving forces behind the daughter's psychological development and the rejuvenation of her own family offers a way out of the darkness of the past.

Like the genre of the *memory play,* these poems often begin with an introduction by the narrator and then unfold in the character's world. Tennessee Williams coined the term in the stage notes to his *The Glass Menagerie* to explain the use of memory as a vehicle for narrative. "The scene is memory and is therefore non-realistic," Williams wrote. He expounds, in a description relevant to Olds's artistry: "Memory takes a lot of poetic license. It omits some details; others are exaggerated, according to the emotional value of the articles it touches, for memory is seated predominantly in the heart. The interior is therefore rather dim and poetic."[3] Olds's details are indeed exaggerated as a means of commenting on their emotional value. Her poems often deal with the concept that the dead remain with the living and frequently describe states of mind in which the past is an almost overwhelming force. As was the case for Emily Dickinson, death and passion are two of Olds's major themes. Death is usually as a symbol for the angst of memory, particularly as it relates to childhood and love, although unlike Dickinson's, Olds's portrayals of sexual love are at times somewhat graphic.

Olds's emotional correlatives are extremely personal, a typical trait of the confessional poets; yet she taps into a collective sense of experience for North American suburbanites. Her poems speak to familiar domestic experiences and locations—napping in the family living room, making out in the front seat of a car, returning from a long road trip with children in the backseat—even if these are invested with considerably more drama than such seemingly homey and ordinary situations would suggest. This penchant for unlikely but honest melodrama has polarized reviewers. While some value her forthright descriptions of family life and sexuality and her sympathy for victims, other see her work as profane, sometimes pornographic, self-indulgent, self-pitying, and obsessed with violence. William Logan, for example, takes issue with Olds's emphasis on family disharmony:

> Readers now thumb through Olds to get to the good parts, as teenagers a generation ago furtively paged through their parents' copy of Peyton Place. She trades in shameless prose chopped up into lines of poetry, lurid as a tabloid, returning to the primal scene more often than a therapist: her cold, sadistic father; her cold, masochistic mother; the chair her parents tied her to; the birth of her children; her nipples; and always, always, her marriage bed. If someone is raped in her apartment building, we never hear about the victim. We're told instead about Olds having sex the next day. . . .

> Olds may someday become the laureate of the bedroom; but for all her radical pretense, she's a homely Redbook moralist, believing in motherhood, family, and honey on her nipples. By the time she's reduced to giving sex tips, or calling her husband's member "the errless digit," all her shallow pretense is greedily on display.[4]

Adam Kirsch, whose review of *Blood, Tin, Straw* is thorough but not very kind to Olds overall, opined that "no one who really believed in the sheer corporeality of sex and birth, out of a pre-Christian paganism or a post-Christian materialism, would write about them with such pointed prurience. Olds's aim is not clarity, but blasphemy." Nevertheless Kirsch provided a good summary of the forces in her work:

> Olds warms to this role [of the blasphemer], the naughty child, and tries by increase of naughtiness to bring on some cataclysm in which either she of the godlike enemy would be destroyed. That enemy is a whole complex of political, social, and religious attitudes that devalue sexuality and oppress women, often represented by her own alcoholic father, the demon of her unhappy childhood. The most naughty thing, of course, is sex; and the only thing naughtier than sex is sex with one's parents or children. In Olds's work, every permutation of this sin is played out. She imagines her parents having sex, imagines having sex with her parents, imagines her children sexually.[5]

Although this is an overview of Olds's work, Kirsch's emphasis on the "naughty" Olds misses two of the most pertinent facets of her poetry: first, extreme vision (besides being good entertainment) is an examination of human nature when reduced to its most primal, and thus most revealed, self; and second, the prevalence of sex is not simply, as Logan asserts, "prurient, anatomical detail the Greek philosophers would have killed for," but also an evocation of the important natural cycle that allows the species to grow and expand, emotionally as well as literally. Like Walt Whitman, Olds is a poet who uses these extremes to encourage evolution. As Carolyne Wright has written: "By confronting her own 'darkness' fairly, Olds has affirmed the humanity of those who engendered that darkness, and shown herself, in these days of sensationalized telling-all for lucrative book contracts, to be a poet of affirmation."[6] Tony Hoagland also came to Olds's defense against critics such as Kirsch: "Isn't this [telling all], not prurience, but empathy, recognition, curiosity, and courage? Isn't one job of the artist to imagine his way vividly into the unfashionable nooks and crannies of experience, the central meaning of the real? . . . To me, this is not Olds' 'prurient' imagination, but the real human story, embedded in myth and poetry, the tangle of primal psychological relationships."[7] This dichotomy of opinions, either of which could be successfully defended, actually speaks to Olds's breadth and power as a poet. She is a protean writer who tirelessly investigates the concealed, indecorous aspects of human nature with honesty and pathos at the same time that she is a sexually explicit provocateur who garners attention by embracing taboos.

Olds's combination of the personal and the geopolitical can appear off-putting when, for instance, resentment over childhood punishment turns into a comparison between the speaker and the victims of war. In "The Takers" and "The Pact," two poems from *The Dead and the Living,* the cruelty of the parents passes to their offspring. Psychic violence then manifests in the children as violence, both imagined and real. In "The Takers" at a time when both girls are children, the narrator's older sister enters her room and pins her to her bed. She "sat astride me, squeezed me with her knees," the daughter says, "held her thumbnails to the skin of my wrists and / peed on me" (45). The daughter recalls the event with the details of trauma—the silence, her sister's "dark face above me / gleaming in the shadows," the smell of the urine, "my small / pelvis wet." As typical of Olds's style, the narrator then compares her experience with Adolf Hitler's invasion of Paris in June 1940; the poem ends on a slight misquote of Hitler's alleged comment upon seeing Napoleon's tomb: "*This is the / finest moment of my life.*" What at first might appear to be exaggeration and self-indulgence is actually a synecdoche of the great brutal forces of the world. As the child does, so too the dictator. Both act with cruelty to fuel their damaged egos. It would be easy to blame Olds, as some do, for comparing her own personal experiences of a long-ago family trauma with the brutality of dictators and the mendacity of disgraced presidents. But Olds is writing in a culture milieu and society obsessed with the abuses of power.

"The Pact," likewise, examines the psychological trajectory of familial dysfunction. The two children of "that house where Father staggered with the / Thanksgiving knife, where Mother wept at / noon into her one ounce of / cottage cheese" mirror their parents as they play with dolls, bathing and swaddling them as "if we had made a / pact of silence and safety." In the gulf opened by their parents' neglect and pain, the daughter and her sister become the parents, fulfilling their emotional needs by succoring the imaginary lives of dolls. However because the domestic sphere is poisoned, the two sisters go through the motions of drowning and burning their toy children. In this way they carry forward their parents' damage into their own parenting. Olds is commenting about the ways in which the home creates the world of adult behavior. That the child is mother to the woman is one of her favorite themes. And what might appear self-indulgent could arguably be a method of reifying the intense feelings that people, particularly children, experience during times of familial stress. In other words Olds tends to use exaggerated language because the emotions people experience while dealing with family are often exaggerated. This incentive to amplify is most overt during recollections of childhood, but Olds also uses the tropes to describe parent characters bravely battling illness or on the brink of death.

Thus at this point it would be appropriate to return to the problems with the term *confessional* as it is applied to Olds and others. The first acknowledged work of modern confessional literature is Delmore Schwartz's story "In Dreams Begin Responsibilities."[8] The title is taken from an epigraph to W. B. Yeats's 1914 collection *Responsibilities and Other Poems* (Yeats is also a poet sometimes labeled confessional), attributed simply and enigmatically to "An Old Play." Schwartz's 1937 story holds all the basic components of the confessional mode: family dysfunction, humiliation, the promise of future instability, melodrama, the narrator implicitly psychoanalyzing himself, and the gratuitous metaphoric construction that so often accompanies this narrative recipe. The story is a relatively simple first-person account of an early date between the narrator's father and mother—the narrator, a young man, actually looks back into the past and relates what he sees; he has, in this circumstance, a preternatural (and in some ways unfair) ability to interpret and analyze his parents' moods and emotions. His insight is born, the reader understands, from the narrator's own painful childhood memories, which are simultaneously in the past and in the future as the story is being told. Such a conundrum of time is essential to the confessional mode, which must tread heavily both in the past and the future-anterior, or the future as imagined in the present as if it had already happened. The parents are themselves young, yet to be ravaged by the psychological forces of personality, culture, and fate. They are described in terms that make clear their impending dysfunction. Responsibilities begin with the dreams of young, ideological people, the narrative implies, and the failure to live up to these responsibilities destroys everything that follows. Schwartz codified the basic template of twentieth-century confessionalism (a mode already practiced by any number of writers from Shakespeare to Tennessee Williams) as it would be thereafter practiced by poets, novelists, filmmakers, talk show hosts, and reality television producers.

In their introduction to *The Selected Poems of Anne Sexton,* Diane Wood Middlebrook and Diana Hume George provide the generally accepted definition of confessionalism as it pertains to poetry: "Confessional poetry seemed to constitute a break with poetic tradition, dispensing with the stance of authorial distance that characterized 'high poetry' and widening the scope of permissible subject matter to include intimate and disturbing experiences formerly classified as too personal—sometimes too embarrassing—for serious art. Private and taboo subject matter understood in psychological terms gave confessional poetry its distinctive character."[9] Virtually any poem in the confessional mode (because it is actually a mode and not limited to any one genre) contain a revelation of a painful experience or secret, something that most people would find embarrassing to discuss. This particular autobiographical aspect of confessionalism that seems to alienate so many also lends authenticity to the narrations. It is easy to believe, for instance, that a child might be tied to a chair by her parents or that a mother might climb on top of her sleeping child to weep (both narrative events in Olds's poems) or any number of likely but dramatic scenarios that are the province of hidden experience. For this reason alone, scene and narration are important to the confessional poem, with the proviso that many of the finest confessional poems are predicated upon pure sensation or explicate emotion, no matter how conceivably prurient. Again private life is linked to public life in a manner that dramatizes the link between them. This should be read as a strength of the confessional aesthetic. As Anis Shivani has written, echoing a frequent complaint about contemporary poetry: "Poets have forsaken keen knowledge of public figures, public events, and public history, so that even when forced on occasion to confront a large-scale tragedy (usually it is this which obliges them to pen a few lines to 'deal with' the crisis, rather than a Whitmanesque exposition that embraces the good and the bad, before calamity strikes), they approach it through the screen of private experience."[10] The same cannot be said of Olds's poetry.

In some respects Olds redefines the confessional aesthetic—and thus she could be considered a postconfessional poet. Her postconfessional lyrics unapologetically celebrate a number of themes that other confessional poets, deliberately or not, use to denote a fallen America. These themes include sexuality, traditional motherhood, and the grotesquerie of the body. Olds values sex and the body, even in their grotesque or abject aspects. In other respects, too, she redefines the politics of the confessional. Her narratives and meditations are sometimes overtly feminist. At other times, however, the poet celebrates the traditional role of motherhood and self-negation in favor of her children. Thus, particularly thematically, the daughter returns to a gender dynamic more generally associated with older generations and less so with the generations of women post-second-wave feminism. Olds reifies and gives voice to a number of human experiences, good and bad, tragic and joyous, that are familiar in Western culture. The veneer of civility and art that often separates expression from reality is annulled in her verse, and what the reader receives is the real inner self of the poet, for better or worse. This vantage on the human, however, is not always politically correct. Males of all ages are associated with violence, strength, growth, ambition, and power; females of all ages are associated with nascent sexuality (for the young), mature sexuality (for the adult), motherhood, and rituals of nurturing, growth, and transcendence. At the same time, Olds's position as narrator privileges a feminine perspective on culture, and she is one of the most unflinching and outspoken poets on the issue of violence toward women and children.

Some Notes on Style

Despite her generally plainspoken style, Olds is also a poet of wit and symbolism. In describing the rather rough tucking in she received from her mother ("At Night," *OST* 25), the daughter's iambic tetrameter accentuates the "jamming motion" of the mother's fingers with the adroit and startling use of alliteration and assonance, punctuating the overall description of the bed accoutrements with harsh consonant sounds and a mix of aspirants and percussives:

> her fingertips
> against the swag of sheets and blankets
> hanging down, where the acme angle of the
> Sealy Posturepedic met
> the zenith angle of the box spring.

Additionally in this instance Olds utilizes everyday products of capitalism as symbols of violent suburban ennui. The mother here treats her children with such accidental but unstinting brutality that even while tucking them into bed she causes them harm.

Olds's use of imagery, particularly surreal images, is deft and startling. For instance in "Good Measure" (*OST* 67), the emotional force of the mother is rendered through complex free association: "she was a gurdy / of atoms swinging from each other's elbows," to which the speaker joins "a force of hurdy wolvine cream." A gurdy by itself is a large drum used to haul fishing lines and nets aboard commercial fishing vessels, but the word is virtually always used as part of the name of a hand-cranked musical instrument of medieval origin, the hurdy-gurdy. Olds splits this compound noun between two lines, leaving the questions of how or why this instrument is suspended between the mother's "elbows" deliberately dreamlike and ambiguous. Other examples illustrate a nearly metaphysical, language-oriented aesthetic. In "The Try-Outs" (*BTS* 67) housework is described as "matter / and dirt-on-matter squealing, the dust-rings of / Saturn grating on each other," while in "The Older" (*TUR* 68), the aging female body is rendered alien and yet beautiful through a series of brief, multisyllabic phrases that stand out because of their unlikely unions of adjectives, nouns, and verbs: "witherly and scrawny," "silvery witheriness," "skin thinning," "ruched wraith," "a wrinkle of smoke."

Grammarians will note that Olds often uses what composition instructors call a comma splice. Sentences do not end with a period but stream down the page as a series of clauses linked by commas. Certainly someone with Olds's educational pedigree understands that this is a grammatical error. However, her emphasis is on phrases rather than on sentence structure. Without the grammatical endstop of a period, ideas conjoin across the comma splice, essentially creating stream-of-consciousness poetry through the deliberate misuse of punctuation.

Another important aspect of Olds's poetry is the relationship between poems in the collections. As a brief example, four poems in *The Dead and the Living*—"The Victims" (34), "The Forms" (35), "The Departure" (36), and "Burn Center" (37)—form a unit of discourse in which the daughter negotiates her own conflicted feelings about her parents. Throughout her collections Olds orders her poems carefully so as to create correspondences within individual sections and within the book as a whole. In "The Victims" the character of the father, now finally divorced from the mother, becomes an analogue to Richard Nixon as he left the South Lawn of the White House via helicopter upon his resignation. The daughter unabashedly revels in the father's fall from grace when he loses his job and all the accoutrements of business, including the "lunches with three double bourbons," and even his suits, "those dark / carcasses hung in your closet." Ultimately, the Father is reduced in the daughter's vision to a member of the lowest economic class in the capitalist worldview, the "bums in doorways, the white / slugs of their bodies gleaming." As a counterpoint the mother in "The Forms," the next poem in the suite, is implicitly valorized ("I always had the feeling my mother would / die for us, jump into a fire . . . her hair burning like / a halo") and excused for her own emotional turmoil and self-concern ("but in life as it was / she had to put herself / first"). Then the father is once again denigrated in "The Departure" when he is compared to Reza Pahlavi, the former Shah of Iran, who treats his subjects with the same imperial distance with which the father treated his family. "You knew us no more than he knew them," the daughter says, "his lowest subjects, his servants, and we were / silent before you like that." Such ordering is important to Olds's overall commentary and creates arcs of meaning, intertwining symbols, and a subtle emotional thrust.

Likewise Olds is one of the few contemporary poets who works in extended narrative sequences. These sequences come in one of two forms: brief narratives of lyrical poems that sketch a single speaker's experiences (like the sequence in the previous paragraph) and extended narratives that develop exclusively across entire collections. Specifically two of Olds's books, *The Father* and *Stag's Leap,* are built around cohesive arcs that reveal a single dramatic storyline. Each one is essentially a novel in verse. Both present their stories in semichronological tableaus, vignettes, and memory poems that create an effect much like snapshots in a family album; large sections of the narratives are absent or merely alluded to, and the balance between exposition and revelation is often canted toward moments of disclosure without a backstory. Yet what might appear to be a weakness inherent in the genre actually works well in a narrative medium predicated upon recollection: the abbreviated, unconnected nature of the lyric creates a pattern of narrative much like actual memory. Some memories are clearer and stronger than others, even if these seem inconsequential, while others, obviously important, are abstract as if shrouded by distance. Some memories suggest experiences, while others narrate the past with clarity. And some memories recur, arriving from earlier incarnations in Olds's canon, while yet others rise once and then disappear. In this way Olds reenacts the actual experience of memory, with all its random associations and illogical appearances, while at the same time refining experience into cogent narrative sequences.

In addition, even within individual sections in her books, Olds tends to pair poems together, one responding to the other on facing or following pages. Sometimes these companion poems offer alternative, even contradictory, versions of the same subject; sometimes they offer complementary images and ideas; sometimes they exhibit nuances or expansions of the previous poem. As prime examples "Late" (*SS* 30) and "The Housewives Watching Morning TV" (*SS* 31) offer two versions of the same social/psychological/biological issue: the difference in the ways men and women deal with women's rights. The central image that both poems share is of fire. In "Late" the evening mist is "like some from a battle." The battle being evoked is the battle of the sexes, fought in public debates, in the media, and in colleges and workplaces throughout the 1960s and 1970s. The battlefield is the lawns and houses of suburbia. The speaker resents the patriarchal power and relative domestic weakness of women, but her reaction is sexual, desirous. She wants to "bite their mouths and feel their hard cocks against me," she says, even though she admits her own need to break free from the laundry duties and childrearing obligations of the domestic sphere. In the next line, she is longing for greatness. She understands that violent confrontation is anathema to her character. "The only way out is through / fire," the speaker says, but she is not a warrior: "I do not want a single / hair of a single head singed." In "The Housewives Watching Morning TV," the first seventeen lines are pure reportage of an assistant fire commissioner on a morning talk show. The subject of the program is the difference between fires set by men—either pathological arsonists who light fires for sexual gratification or those "normal arsonists"—and those more delicate "grudge" fires set by women: "tie a pair of nylons / on a neighbor's doorknob, set them on fire." Men's fires last longer and are more effective, destroy more, kill more. The women stand in a room "littered like public *I* hallways"—symbolizing the panoptic nature of their social lives—as they "lean like sacks against the walls," listening powerlessly to the fire marshal. Yet inside the women smolder, and the smoke rises through their mouths, foreshadowing the spoken word of feminist conflagration. It is interesting to note that Olds ends on a rare literary allusion; the smoke is dark as the bile of Gustav Flaubert's famously adulterous and ultimately suicidal Emma Bovary. Olds's meaning here is ambiguous as is the future imagined by the poem, but the poet seems to imply that the life of the housewife is perilous for men and women alike as the fires of both genders threaten to consume them. This is the final image of the poem and a rare literary allusion for a poet who focuses so intently upon contemporary experience. In an interview with Amy Hempel for *Bomb* magazine, Olds explained her vision of art, which seems like an interesting way to introduce her poetry:

> It has always seemed so obvious and powerfully true that art and life are incredibly different from each other. Flesh is flesh. A poem is breath in the air. Or it's ink and paper. It's standing for a heart and a mind. And I go to people's poems to learn about the heart and the mind, and to be less lonely as a human being, and to have fun. And maybe people go to poetry partly to find out what we're really like, to find out how bad we really are, how essential it is that we change while there's still time, maybe, to change. But a day in a life and a poem about that day, there's something profoundly different. Now, when I was a child, the bread was the flesh of Christ. I ate the ration stamps, I ate the communion wafer. And now, when I go to poems, I am hoping to be changed, to learn something about sexual love, or birth, or the joy or rage of some particular person or group—maybe very different from me or mine—while at the same time I am experiencing the physical pleasure of the beat, tone, music, shape, the whole intricate body of the poem and spirit of the speaker. So that, while one is still alive, one can feel, and know, as much as possible, so as to be fully alive.[11]

CHAPTER 2

Manifestos

Olds has occasionally written metapoetry, joining a tradition as old as Horace's original *Ars Poetica,* a lengthy verse epistle on the correct and incorrect techniques of poetry written in the first century B.C.E. Horace's instructions include proper decorum, subject, meter, style, and imagery. His aim was codification of the rules for Augustan poetry and the edification of a particular literal-minded Roman senator. Yet he also initiated a genre with a long line of descendants stretching across the ages, with literally hundreds of poems about the art of poetry. Perhaps the best-known contemporary metapoem is Archibald MacLeish's aptly titled "Ars Poetica," with its famous dictum, "A poem should not mean / But be." While Olds's language is often evocative and symbolic (and thus manages to *be* with all its indefinable quality), her poetry is generally polemical and timely (and thus *means* in an accessible manner). In a quartet of *ars poeticas* from three different books—"Satan Says" (*SS* 3), "I Go Back to May 1937" (*TGC* 23), "Poem to the Reader" (*BTS* 22), and "Take the I Out" (*BTS* 43)—Olds lays out blueprints, sometimes after the fact, for her poetic output. However, following the confessional aesthetic, her focus never strays far from the author herself, and particularly her reasons for writing, as the main subject, and so these four poems can also be read as manifestos, or public declarations of her poetic policies and aims. Olds's *ars poeticas* also concern the artistry of language and the possibility of self-destruction through expression.

Olds's debut collection, *Satan Says,* sprang onto the national poetry scene in 1980 as the inaugural winner of the Poetry Center Book Award from San Francisco State University and helped to establish her national reputation. The titular poem, "Satan Says," is, deliberately or not, an explication of the themes Olds has explored throughout her career. It represents a girl's entry into adolescence and the sundering of parental control, particularly over female sexuality, through a treacherous pact with the devil. As with most of her poetry, it is difficult to mistake its meaning, especially when Olds taps into the familiar supernatural genre of the bewitched child. Taking as its historical precedent the Salem witch trials, commercially successful fiction such as William Peter Blatty's *The Exorcist* (and its film adaptation) reinforced the symbolic notion of preadolescent girls as possessed by demonic, sexualized madness. "Satan Says" plays with this same topos, albeit more overtly and more purposefully.

The narrator (a juvenile version of the daughter) is locked in a prelapsarian but claustrophobic state of innocence symbolized by a child's jewelry box. As with much of Olds's poetry, the self-destructive aspect of her escape is not ironic; her characters actively seek out experience, well aware of the hazards of expression, to the point of self-destruction. "I guess I am someone who likes to push to the edge of what it is OK to have in a poem," Olds has said. "That is my mischievous side, to teeter on the edge of good taste, on what is permissible."[1] Also typical of Olds's poetry, the poem itself is an argument; individual symbols in "Satan Says" represent those cultural forces that constrain young women, and the poem implicitly argues for their dissolution. The box itself is decorated with overt Christian symbolism ("shepherds pasted onto / the central panel between carvings") and images of childlike innocence ("a gold, heart-shaped lock"). Typical of Olds's unflinching phallocentrism, there is "no key" to the box—a heavy-handed reminder that the narrator is referring to putative virginity. Such allusions are arguably shocking, even by the comparatively loose standards of expression since modernism, and this is also part of Olds's art: the reader is forced to confront biological and psychological forces that shape culture, even those most contained. Olds's technique combines dissent and dark humor even as she acknowledges (as a woman who came of age in the turbulent political climate of the 1960s) the dangers of protest. Thus the entry of "Satan," who acts very much as the Devil should, promising to facilitate the daughter's escape, but only on the condition that she perform the first and in some ways most profound of childhood sins: the degradation of the parents. Profanity, the use of which is often taboo and a rite of passage in American childhood, are magic words the daughter uses to break free. These resonances of childhood in America are subtle. Unlike with many English-language poets, the art and artifice of language is, at best, a tertiary theme in Olds's canon amid concerns about sexuality, violence toward women, neglect of children, love, and family relationships—except in the case of "Satan Says," which is a poem predicated upon the relationship between language and power. Language is privileged as a means of escaping psychological trauma. Yet "Satan Says" is as much concerned with the violence of language as it is a celebration of liberation through expression, and one cannot achieve psychic freedom through speech without collateral damage to those one speaks about. For this reason the Devil is the necessary provocateur. A Prometheus of the word, he leads the daughter through the transgressive ritual that signals the onset of adolescence.

> Satan
> comes to me in the locked box
> and says, I'll get you out. Say
> My father is a shit. I say
> my father is a shit and Satan
> laughs and says, *It's opening.*

This is grotesque and even carnivalesque. Gender and family roles are upended, and the normative world is challenged through black humor. Social norms are specifically subverted. For the narrator transgression equals evolution as her "spine uncurls" with all the vernacular implications of growing a spine, even as the imagery is distinctly alien and impetus the least human expression; however, despite the vernacular expression for finding one's inner strength, the unfurling spine is a distinctly alien evocation—as human spines do not generally move this way—which emphasizes the oneiric situation of the poem. "Shit. Death. Fuck the father" births a triumphal manifestation of abjection. Excrement and morbidity are willfully embraced in a prurient expression of the Electra complex. The utterance "Fuck the father" can be read simply as an adolescent slur, but when put into the context of Olds's canon, particularly the midcareer collections, the sexual desire for the father character gains thematic prominence. It should be noted that this apparently incestuous impulse is actually an unfulfilled need for attention from an emotionally distant patriarch, not true sexual desire. Nevertheless there is something cathartic in the father-cum-lover, and Satan can turn to a clichéd paternal platitude for comfort: "*Don't you feel a lot better?*" Always in the family poems adolescent discovery provides the template for taboo unveiling that strains but fails to find catharsis.

As Olds's later poetry makes apparent, her overarching theme is the revelation of the painful yet occasionally triumphant past. Since the lyrical innovations of the romantics, most Western poetry is based upon snippets of memory reconfigured as interior dialogue. Olds continues this tradition: "I'm trying to say what happened to us," the narrator states in *Satan Says*, "in the lost past." As exemplified in Delmore Schwartz's "In Dreams Begin Responsibilities," notions of a "lost past" are part of the confessional gestalt, and revision through constructed memory is an essential component. Schwartz's innovation allows, even encourages, memory's protean illogic to form commentary. Satan becomes the antihero of illogic, the Prince of Darkness, the dictator of the unconscious, who breaches the barrier to the ultimate taboo (*"Say: the father's cock, the mother's / cunt"*) until the box finally breaks open. It is here that the poem turns strangely to images that resemble the birth canal. Within the context of a poem as profane as "Satan Says," in which desecrations of the parents' genitalia are central to the theme of sundered innocence, the birth canal metaphor makes perverse sense.

Yet there is a surprise twist in the narrative: "Oh no," the narrator realizes as Satan begins his final deception. "I loved / them, too." The lid hinges closed; Satan escapes through the keyhole and seals the woman child in her box of sins with the wax of his tongue. Captured in the climate of cold and dark (new elements in the box), the narrator huddles against the "ballerina pin / with a ruby eye" as if it is a hearth fire, the first usage of fire as a leitmotif in Olds's oeuvre. The ballerina represents the rarified image of girlhood, and against this the real girl, trapped by the sins of her angers and longings, warms herself. Olds's narrator often exhibits this level of self-abasement; through her own self-portrayals, in her own words, the daughter repeats this basic pattern of unveiling and self-torment. Walter E. Lewellan argues that the "ruby eye" represents rose of Sharon, a common name for a type of flowering plant found throughout the world and, interestingly, in the Song of Solomon: "I am the rose of Sharon, and the lily of the valleys. / As the lily among thorns, so is my love among the daughters." Ironically the rose of Sharon surrounds the daughter with red, the color of shame. Lewellan has written: "Like reading the Song of Solomon, we could be reading a language that exceeds the limits of propriety. . . . The crude, reductive violence of banal obscenities forms a kind of visual and tonal maze: shit, fuck, cock, cunt, come. These words are all worked on Satan's waxy tongue; they all are repeated by the speaker—except 'come.' She does not come. She does not come out: desire to resist, resistance to desire. It is also about the fall of 'Sharon.' She is dead already, in her coffin, in the tomb: or within the walls of a cedar house."[2] It should be noted, however, that the motifs of "Satan Says" are open to interpretation. As Sybil Estess stated, "Olds's poetry declines Satan's offer to disparage any aspect of her life."[3] One cannot erase hurt simply by cursing it, and to be caught in Satan's mouth is to lose the power of imagination. Olds's poems, according to Estess, are the work of a survivor. They reflect childhood pain overcome by adult joy. Olds is matter-of-fact rather than self-pitying. Hate can be transformed into understanding, even pity, by perseverance. Such a perspective illustrates an aspect of Olds's art that her detractors often overlook, namely, the perception of strength. What appears to be weakness—symbolized by the victory of Satan—is actually a refusal to destroy oneself. The poet remains in the sphere of imagination, though this reading ignores the tragic denouement of Satan's trickery. At times, perhaps accidentally, Olds is perceived as a spokeswoman for the downtrodden because she is willing to write about the forbidden. She follows a poetic principle she has attributed to Muriel Rukeyser: "write about what they tell you to forget, write about what they tell you to forget, write about what they tell you to forget."[4] She is unafraid of probing the Jungian shadow realms, a function best suited to the confessional I. All these issues are engaged in Olds's first manifesto: family and sex (both good and bad), women's issues, oedipal dysfunction of the patriarchal middle-class family, the quest for health and absolution, the freedom of transgression, and the complex relationship these forces have to expression.

"Satan Says" also serves the purpose of exposition. It is through these first brief, obscene, oblique allusions that readers are introduced to the major players in Olds's poetry: the father and the mother. The daughter's mission is to reveal these two characters, even down to the indecorous intimacies of family life. Much of Olds's poetry is occupied with a father who is, in virtually every regard, a "shit." Less often portrayed but nevertheless important, the mother reverses the expected norms of motherhood: she is the weaker, more codependent of the two parents, and she is portrayed first with rage, then pity, then forgiveness, a state granted the father only provisionally and only by implication.

In Olds's extended family drama, which rivals those of Eugene O'Neill or William Faulkner for psychological relevance, the first-person speaker is designated as the daughter. In fact the first section of *Satan Says* is titled "Daughter." Her role as the progeny, the victim, and the unflinching judge of the mother and father (a critique bordering on character assassination) is the single greatest agon in Olds's oeuvre. The first-person narrator consistently battles memories of an abusive childhood of emotional rather than physical violence, marked by alcoholism and emotional distance. The daughter reenacts the dysfunction between her parents, and while she speaks always as an adult, using a mature vocabulary and diction, her recollections are retold with the exaggeration of a child. The father in particular is limned throughout the poems in hyperbolic terms: he is, for instance, compared to a Roman mythic character who devours his own children, the fire of the cosmos, and a light that suffuses the very atmosphere as he dies in her seminal book *The Father*. While the sexual abuse implied in "Satan Says" is never directly confirmed, allusions to abuse, promiscuity, and incest form leitmotifs throughout Olds's work. Her purpose in these instances seems to be to shock the reader into attention and to imply the damage done by family dysfunction. "Satan Says," with its archetypal duality between good and evil and its symbolic originary story, is a creation myth of sorts, unmistakably parallel to the myth of Pandora.

Pandora, as portrayed by Hesiod in both *The Theogony* and *Works and Days,* was the first woman. She was forged by Hephaestus from the earth and was divinely beautiful. She was clothed in a silver gown loomed by Athena and draped with golden jewelry gifted by either the Graces or Persuasion and Charity, depending on the version of the myth. Each of the gods placed a torment in a jar (not a box as is commonly portrayed in English illustrations), and Pandora was banished to the earth. When Pandora opened the jar, the torments were let loose on earth as a punishment to humanity for accepting the gift of fire from the Titan Prometheus and have tormented humanity ever since. Appropriating the topos, "Satan Says" refashions an allegory of personal, rather than mythic, proportions. Pandora's mistake was simple curiosity, while the daughter's mistake is deliberately transgressive. And while the daughter's box is resealed, her psyche, which by the end of the poem has been unhinged by "the fire, the suddenly discovered knowledge of love" of poetry, can, like Pandora's jar, never be closed. It is the final irony of the poem, which sometimes occurs in the confessional mode, when the author confesses to the dangers of understanding. What is most important in this final turn is the "knowledge of love," a phrase evocative of many things—the discovery of sexuality, the development of a girl into a woman, and, quite overtly, the love of creative expression. "Satan Says" finally is a polemic about the necessity of expression and the primacy of visceral experience. And it is a frank admission that such revelation is not a panacea—is, in fact, a danger.

As if to exemplify the paradox of maturity above, "I Go Back to May 1937" is a manifesto to exploit the family agon without apology. In this brief lyric, the daughter lays out her plans to use her own family history, particularly the parents' story, to craft her poetry. It will not be a cheerful retelling. The setting is a spring afternoon on her parents' college campus. They are young, naïve and unsullied, but the mise-en-scène is filled with auguries of violence. Red tiles "glint like bent / plates of blood" over the father's head. Opposite him the mother, "with a few light books at her hip," stands before a vaguely phallic "pillar made of tiny bricks," having just passed through a wrought-iron gate that was her only opening to the world. She can still turn back, but it is obvious that she will not. Her own subsumed psychic violence, which transforms through Olds's semilinear poetic history into codependence and overwhelming self-pity (she literally crawls into her daughter's bed and weeps on top of her), burns on the arrowhead tips of the iron gate. The daughter perceives the coming family conflagration to be burning like "sword-tips aglow in the May air." Just like these omens of the optic nerve of the mind, the characters are about to be turned inside out. The tragedy, in a typical move for Olds, turns to overt commentary: "They are kids, they are dumb, all they know is they are / innocent, they would never hurt anybody." Into this imagined future-anterior landscape, the daughter briefly intrudes, or at least tries to intrude, with an injunction to her parents to "stop," though she knows they will not. This simple declaration accentuates the frustration expressed in the anaphora:

> you are going to do things
> you cannot imagine you would ever do,
> you are going to do bad things to children,
> you are going to suffer in ways you have not heard of,
> you are going to want to die.

In moments such as these one is tempted to deride Olds for her dramatic treatment of what Adam Kirsch pejoratively deems "the videotape of life played back at full volume."[5] These are first world problems, tragedies created by selfish, self-indulgent middle-class people with access to education, food, money, houses, cars, and alcohol. The damage they inflict upon the world is no more tangible than any booze-soaked, exaggerated plaint about myopic family dysfunction, and yet these are people whom Olds portrays with a sense of violence and pathos appropriate to high tragedy. The daughter assumes the role of omniscient narrator, capable of changing and predicting history; she is better in both degree and kind to the people she is writing about, people who, not incidentally, gave her birth. This apparently unexamined irony that seems to provoke some of Olds's critics. Near the end of his review, Kirsch succinctly criticizes Olds's naked revelations, which he considers rebellion without artistry: "Olds's blasphemies and affirmations are always in deadly earnest, which is why they are devoid of two of the most appealing qualities of Plath's verse: wit and artifice."[6] Similarly Ken Tucker criticizes the meagerness of Olds's subject matter: "We find the poet struggling, like a sort of metrical Martha Stewart, to make the earthily mundane blossom into flowery profundity."[7]

A champion of Olds, on the other hand, would point out that much personal tragedy is a product of perception, that many of us experience a depth of emotional upheaval from just such unhealthy families, and that the audience, rightly or wrongly, actually enjoys the melodrama. Peter Redgrove said of Olds's work that "every poem is a wonder—strong, actual, unsentimental and without bullshit—in a world glowing with solid reality."[8] Her focus on reality rather than wit and artifice can also be read as a strength, and Olds's sense of melodrama, particularly when dealing with portrayals of the body and sexuality, resonates with many readers, who seem to appreciate her frank discourse.

Freshness is the root of Olds's appeal. She has the ability to surprise with turns of phrase, insights into the human condition, and nuanced metaphorical constructions built around common experience. At the same time, what most renders her relevant is an aspect of the confessional mode that is often overlooked: the heightened sense of personal drama that reflects the larger political forces in the world. Confessional lyric tends toward insularity, self-indulgence, and psychological issues particular to the poet, and yet, at the same time, the form often speaks to central human experiences such as family life. For Olds the trauma of childhood is an implicit call to action; in "I Go Back to May 1937," she has said very simply:

> . . . I
> take them up like the male and female
> paper dolls and bang them together
> at the hips, like chips of flint, as if to
> strike sparks from them, I say
> Do what you are going to do, and I will tell about it.

As with "Satan Says," language is the arbitrator of experience and revelation equals precarious but necessary freedom.

In "Possessed" the daughter provides a more explicated version of this conflict. "Your bodies are before me / at all times," she says. Here she is apostrophizing the parents, but her real audience is the readership who has become familiar with the poet's childhood, her obsession with childhood generally, and the phobias and neuroses of the father and mother characters. To this end the daughter metaphorizes her parents into the cosmic ("the stars of your teeth"); the commercial ("blue that reflects from the knife blade"); the literal ("dead cigars and / Chanel in the mink"); the natural (symbolized by the "slow stopped bear tread" of the father and the description of the mother as a "quick fox, her nails on the ice"); and the deep-seated emotional expressed as abstraction ("I dream the inner parts of your bodies, the / coils of your bowels like smoke"). "Possessed" is an expressionistic catalog of the world as seen through the eyes of the possessed. It describes a form of demonic possession in which every person, every experience, is predicated upon the need for parental affection. "Never having had you," the daughter says, "I cannot let you go."

Olds's third ars poetica, "Poem to the Reader," comes relatively late in her career, at least for a declaration of poetic interest. But she is a memory poet, after all, and interested in hindsight. "Poem to the Reader" is in a sense a collage of themes and motifs found throughout Olds's work. Three of the major conflicts experienced by the daughter persona—which can be reductively identified as sexuality (good and bad), the joys and psychological dangers of motherhood, and the relationship between poet and reader—are cataloged in the poem. These themes run consecutively, each with its own intertwining section, beginning with her recollections of teen angst and teen sexuality (lines 1–17); childbirth and marriage (17–26); the influence of memory symbolized by death (26–33); questions about the nature of sexuality (33–49); and motherhood (49–66) and finally direct address to the reader (59–66). By 1999, when *Blood, Tin, Straw* was published, Olds had already investigated these conflicts in a number of poems in which sexuality and motherhood are wholesome, healing counterpoints to the gendered politics of the masculine world. The daughter expends a good deal of energy in explaining how she has been wronged by the patriarchy and how procreation mends these wrongs.

"Poem to the Reader" is one of the few instances in Olds's oeuvre when the reader cannot be sure who the speaker is. Is the poet speaking directly to the reader in her own voice, or is the daughter the speaker? Regardless the poem follows a typical paradigm for Olds's confessionalism: she begins with an adolescent admission that discursively expands into the hindsight of adulthood. "Since I was thirteen," the narrator says, "I have wondered who I am." Such declarations are usually the province of the turbulent teenage years, and while such feelings might privately persist, maturity (or at least the general sense that petulant childhood should expire with adulthood) provides a sense of self. But Olds's stagecraft is predicated upon melodramatic unveilings and startling bodily images rooted in adolescence. Questions follow, of the sort one might expect to find in a teenager's diary: "was I nice? / was I evil?" And then, in keeping with Olds's frequent exploration of abjection, readers are reminded of the visceral disgust of the adolescent body, often a metonymy for the fragile psyche:

—then squeeze the sebum out of my
pores, slow thick cold sebum.
Under my skin, female flesh
now lay in packs, hip-flasks of fat.
Out of my mouth came a soil-like smell.

The baldly self-denigrating tone illustrates a typical tack in Olds's rhetorical process: it is not clear that such indelicate specificity actually symbolizes anything other than the narrator's own self-denigration, yet there is something powerfully human in acknowledging the repellant aspects of biology. Oddly in this gestalt, the overpowering force of the patriarchy reasserts itself, and in a moment of painful self-observation, the narrator envisions "my father on the couch, passed / out risen up and walking." This scene is an allusion to "Saturn" (*TGC* 24), a poem in which the daughter imagines her father as the mythical Roman god who devours his children. In this instance the allusion also evokes the father as a Christ figure that has risen as if from the dead, one of many iterations that represent the deific power of the parent to both destroy and comfort the child.

As above, the overarching themes are transgressive, particularly involving sex as a counterpoint to family turmoil. "When I would / touch a boy," the narrator says about her ironic experiences of heaven in the front seat of a car, "I would feel like an archangel / crushed to another archangel." Such lines are an iteration of the quasi-religious iconography found in other poems such as "Animal Music" (*BTS* 6) and "Necking" (*TW* 25), which reflect the reverence for physical gratification distinctive to Olds's artistry. Sexual gratification in Olds's poetry can also be an anodyne for the loss of parental affection, or it can be frank rebellion. Yet in "Poem to the Reader," the adolescent narrator is not ready for the ultimate physical experience, and the couple flies, "wings fiercely shut," into gratification without actual consummation; the focus here is exclusively on the sensual act. Afterward, however, she sees her reflection in a mirror and wonders, "was I bad?" This is the first of several questions about the nature of desire in the poem. What is on the one hand a typically adolescent reaction over sexual propriety (has she sinned in enjoying pleasures of the flesh?) can also be read as a commentary upon female eroticism—the implication seems to be that the self-image reflects shame. It is worthy of note that, at this point in the poem, the narrator turns away from the issue of morality. Instead "Poem to the Reader" memorializes one rite of passage among many others in a young woman's life. What is significant is the focus on sheer physical pleasure and the nearly religious transference that accompanies it. Olds seems to be repudiating the notion that shame must accompany desire.

From here the next natural passage is the marriage bed and childbirth, which, surprisingly, involves no ritual or sacrifice: the narrator says of copulation that "it was just the animal," and she describes the birth process as "the real." Such language brings to mind Jacques Lacan's theory of infant development, also termed the "Real." This is the neonatal developmental stage before language acquisition, when thought and desire are pure experience and the thinker is close to nature and seeks only to quench desire. As Dino Felluga explains:

> The primordial animal need for copulation (for example, when animals are in heat) similarly corresponds to this state of nature. There is a need followed by a search for satisfaction. As far as humans are concerned, however, "the real is impossible," as Lacan was fond of saying. It is impossible in so far as we cannot express it in language because the very entrance

> into language marks our irrevocable separation from the real. Still, the real continues to exert its influence throughout our adult lives since it is the rock against which all our fantasies and linguistic structures ultimately fail.[9]

Having received her Ph.D. when literary theory was in vogue, Olds is almost certainly aware of this connotation. Correspondences to the fullness of procreation are too overt to be missed. Sex, and its wholesome outcome of childbirth and family, completes the desires of the human animal, even if this is beyond expression. At the same time, *real* is a term from common parlance, particularly slang ("get real," "for real," "the real thing," essentially memes connoting the truth). Once again, healthy reality is motherhood. The poem reads:

> I sang, while I tended the children,
> day and night went back to the sealed
> universe of the marriage bed.

She contradicts herself at a point when, in the marriage bed, sex is no longer animal passion but is the presence of love: "I felt / virtuous, stuffed to the spirit-tips with touch." Her environment is "sealed" like the story box in "Satan Says," and yet now it is a "universe" with its expansive sexual experience. Perhaps, she suggests, the animal has been supplanted by the spiritual in the sanctity of marriage. However motherhood—the natural offshoot of marriage—has a cost. Her children, she says, still in the past tense, were weaned from her slowly. And here she utters the first evident statement that the life she describes has dangers too. It is one of several statements in Olds's canon that can be read as an allusion to second-wave feminism:

> I felt I was *nothing* without
> someone in my arms, I was a craving spirit,
> the dead stream along the walls of
> houses and affix themselves to the amber windows.

Her call to action is implicit: without a child or husband, she is a nonentity, and while the poem never becomes polemical, the domestic sphere is portrayed as a landscape flowing with the ghosts of fathers, sons, and lovers. Death is a frequent subject in Olds's poetry, usually associated with warfare and the metaphoric burial of the past.

Tellingly "Poem to the Reader" switches to present ("This morning") and assumes a philosophical but adolescent diction. The narrator wonders if she might receive some "word . . . on who I am" and the nature of her own loving. Such self-actualization questions the purpose of the poem in which recollections of motherhood are held to seemingly impossible standards. Typical of

Olds, imagery and language return to notions of sexual love, deliberately and uncomfortably blurring the boundaries between motherhood and the sexual act; the narrator speaks of "buttoning" (a mother dressing her child) and "unbuttoning" (a wife engaging in seduction), "suckling, and sucking" (allusions to nursing and oral sex), life activities that equate paradoxically to feeding "the hunger of the dead." Once again wit and artifice are secondary to forthright, even blunt expression of intimate experience rendered in the frank rhetoric of obscenities. It is debatable whether or not this is a laudable practice, particularly in meditative verse, and a critic could return to the notion of self-indulgent melodrama, while an apologist could return to the notion of verisimilitude through everyday language. Such readings are subjective, of course, but it is hard to deny the power of the vernacular, the most familiar language, to affect people, and Olds's prominence in the world of poetry seems to support this.

The narrator reaffirms the role of memory somewhat alarmingly when she expresses the "*longing* to give an arm" for the dead (emphasis in the original). In many instances Olds turns to surrealism and abstraction to express heightened emotion; in this instance the image of severed arms sitting on a table as a method of exchange is difficult, perhaps impossible, to parse with any certainty. What Olds seems to be getting at is the necessity of sacrifice, perhaps of motherhood or daughterhood, or even the danger of words. The theme of the self-sacrificing mother, the woman who longs for abjection even as she celebrates child rearing, has been associated with the daughter since her character was introduced; she stands as a counterpoint to the neglectful, self-indulgent mother character. The idea of the mutilated writer, however, is unique to "Poem to the Reader." Elsewhere—most notably in *The Father*—writing is associated with strength and renewal, so the severing of the instruments of writing is both problematic and intriguing in this context.

The poem does not, however, bring this image of severance to fruition and returns to one of Olds's favorite themes. The nature of sexual love is again questioned (what if sex is only hedonism?), utilizing typically pornographic language to describe desire: "the cunt wanting / to swallow, swallow, fiercely sing all / day all night." In "Poem to the Reader," the agon is self-doubt, the possibility that the moral substances of life are illusion, including the moral importance given to bodily urges. To metaphorize this the persona raises the unsettling connection between child rearing and adult sexuality. Motherhood is now questioned (is the act of mothering simply a selfish, self-congratulatory, self-preoccupying indulgence?) through suggestive verbs and unsettling descriptions of its daily activities: "I entered / the baby spoon into the mouth"; "I stroke him now, hours of the night"; I "press my face into the / cool nippleless breast of his buttock"). Oddly this section ends on the notion that a pubic hair on "the / sheet, by the lamp, this morning" becomes animate and "tells it," the story of the biological self, the "soul in hell."

"Poem to the Reader" is a metacritique by the poet of her own best work. She calls into question the voyeuristic relationship the reader has with poetry by breaking the fourth wall and addressing her audience directly.

> So I have set the mouth
> of my iris to the mouth of your iris here
> for this brief kiss.

The readers have been included in the sexualized gestalt. The black opening of the eye symbolizes the conduit through which both author and reader interact, and the metaphysical, symbolic plane in which poetry acts as an alembic for the poet to enter the reader; it is, simply put, the eye of the imagination made visible. The fecund darkness also provides a second mouth through which the poet speaks, and the act of kissing the reader is, rather literally, Olds's displaying her affection. Poetry, she seems to say, is an act of giving and receiving and, like sensuality, an act of love.

"Poem to the Reader" culminates the first section, "Blood," of *Blood, Tin, Straw.* The section comprises typically personal poems focused loosely on the daughter's growing sense of herself as a wife and mother in a world full of danger. Poems in the section, such as "The Promise" (3), "Animal Music" (6), and "After the Rape in Our Building" (13), yoke images, narratives, and metaphors of violence to evocations of romantic and parental love. Poems such as "Bacchanal in Memory" (12) and "When It Comes" (14) explore the unsettling brutality of the sexual act despite its link to the necessary beauty of procreation. "Aspic and Buttermilk" (18), returning to a favorite theme, is framed around the recollection of the father's need to dominate his daughter, this time through the ritual of food; the daughter eats meat, raw meat, which disgusts her father, and he forces her to drink tomato aspic, which looks like "the silt of a wound," and buttermilk, "a joke / on milk, and a joke on butter," as a display of parental power. At the heart of this scenario is the mystery surrounding the "beauty and cruelty" of the family, "more passion for life on almost any / terms than death." This statement could be read as yet another ars poetica for Olds and stands naturally behind other poems of love, disgust, and dysfunction—the meditation upon the brother's near-death from drowning and the father's alcoholic reaction ("Boulder Creek") and a recollection of incestuous arousal walking in upon the Father naked upon the toilet ("Once")—that all cohere in the final refrain of painful self-examination and visceral self-loathing that is "Poem to the Reader." *My family did this to me* is the implication of this poetic essay; *I am a product of these memories and narratives.* Olds explores this basic theme repeatedly throughout her work and yet never resolves the essential conflict at its heart.

Appropriately, then, Olds's fourth manifesto, "Take the I Out," is predicated upon the daughter's painful relationship with her parents. The overarching conceit is an I-beam, the structural steel supports known for their distinctive I shape. I-beams are effective for bearing weight and often form the main support matrix of large buildings. In this poem the parents are the building, and the daughter imagines herself as the support that might have braced the family structure, soaring "between them / like the soul that rushes, back and forth, / between the mother and the father." Olds's concept is an interesting statement also within the construction of the section "Tin" in *Blood, Tin, Straw.* She situated "Take the I Out" between two poems on the subject of (implied) abuse, both with self-evident titles: "The Day They Tied Me Up" (41), referring to the evening when the daughter was punished as a child by being tied to a chair, and "After Punishment Was Done with Me" (44), a poem that uses versions of the *I* pronoun sixteen times. "Take the I Out" forms a link between the two poems, symbolizing the self-infantilizing narrator fixed between two poles of traumatic memory. The daughter is as much an auteur of arrested development as she is a commentator upon family ethos and psychological lineage.

At the same time, the *I* of "Take the I Out" is also a reference to the "confessional I," the typically self-disclosing narrator of the confessional mode, and Olds uses the pronoun seventeen times, as if to remind the reader of her presence in the poem. *I* has several iterations in the poem, such as "I love the I," "I-beam," "I have seen," "Roman numeral I," "*I, I, I, I,*" and "I lay with you," to suggest the multiplicity of perspectives possible from the first-person narrator. Olds may be responding to the current of contemporary poetry in the 1990s, which moved away from the confessional aesthetic and toward conceptions of Language and elliptical poetry, both of which distance the speaker from the poem. In "Take the I Out," Olds implicitly argues for the necessity of personal experience and the priority of the speaker. Her diction is somewhat abstract and free-associative in the poem, and her meaning must be refined from the raw verse as foundries refine metals. The process of smelting pig iron into usable steel becomes a conceit for raising a family. The father, readers find out, was a steel salesman, and his peddling provides "bourbon, and Cream / of Wheat," as well as dresses paid for with his "metal sweat." The I becomes "girders of identity" for this history; thus without the I the relevance of experience is lost. Olds's closing statement in her defense of the personal narrator turns the pronoun distinctly vulnerable.

The *I* is a pine,
resinous, flammable root to crown,
which throws its cones as far as it can in a fire.

Once again the important leitmotif of fire (which represents the emotional turmoil of alcoholism, particularly in the male family members) is present as a symbol for the conflagration of familial emotion and its explosive effect on the environment. Her final argument in her final ars poetica is that the I is necessary but that investigating its strength and source is a perilous undertaking.

Since the first use of the term *confessional* in a 1959 review of W. D. Snodgrass's seminal collection *Heart's Needle,* poets have wished to abandon the idea of the "confessional I" (as did Snodgrass), and critics have debated the legitimacy of the confessional genre itself. However, as is so often the case when critics intend a term pejoratively, its associations take on lives of their own, and in 2001 David Graham and Kate Sontag, editors of the anthology *After Confession: Poetry as Autobiography* (which uses Olds's "Take the I Out" as its first entry), write in their introduction: "More than forty years after the poets and the poetry first tagged 'confessional' ignited critical controversy, American poetry continues to display a notable confessional strain—some would say exhaustively so."[10] *After Confession* reiterates and updates many of the complaints about personal poetry—"hyperprivacy has lost our poetry a readership," Sydney Lea laments.[11] Joan Aleshire argues that the confessional poet, "overwhelmed or intoxicated by the facts of his or her life, lets the facts take over. To say a poem is confessional is to signal a breakdown in judgment and craft."[12] On the flip side, Judith Harris interprets a deeper purpose in the confessional lyric: "In the strong poets like [Linda] McCarriston or Olds, confession is a personal outcry that seeks to address a community's consciousness by conflating the inner domestic realm with broader, historical realities."[13]

Billy Collins takes the middle ground, warning in his essay "My Grandfather's Tackle Box: The Limits of Memory-Driven Poetry" that the "key risk in writing the memory-driven poem is a failure to take advantage of the imaginative liberty that poetry offers."[14] His point (following Richard Hugo's directive in his nonfiction *The Triggering Town*) is that memory begins the poetic process, but then imagination should take over and deliver a better, truer version of the truth than the historical truth by itself. Collins asks, "As long as the poem is a good poem, what's the difference if it is true to fact or not?" If there is a caveat, it is to limit, in Aleshire's words, the facts. But there is one other aspect of the autobiographical poem, namely, the relationship between speaker and listener. Collins uses an anecdote to dramatize the personalizing, dramatizing, and overarching power of poet's past:

> I asked the group [of students] how they would feel if I told them that Sharon Olds's father was not really dead. True, she did devote an entire collection (*The Father*) to her father's dying and death. True, the book is a startling series of poems that pushes the elegy into new psychic territory. But in fact, her father is living in Phoenix where he plays golf three or four times a week with his buddies. Mr. Olds, I happened to know, was a 17 handicap. Even though I presented this as pure hypothesis, I could feel a sudden drop in the room temperature, a barometric shift. The students were more than a little stunned even to have to consider such a possibility.[15]

The moment seems a bit precious, the students a bit too dramatic, for reality, but then again Collins's essay is on the power of imagination to augment experience. More important, he is making an argument for the legitimacy of poetry, confessional poetry in particular. Whether he meant to or not, Collins makes cogent arguments against Olds's detractors and in favor of her primacy as a poet of the modern age. According to the essay, the students "were forced to admit that they also wanted the poems to be true in some reliable and ingenuous sense. When all the chips were pushed into the center of the table, they didn't want to hear about 'the speaker' or 'textual distance.' They wanted to believe in a real Sharon . . . a human voice."[16]

CHAPTER 3

The Father Poems

It is not a very flattering portrait.

> My da on his elegant vegetarian ankles
> drank his supper. Like other dinosaurs
> massive, meaty, made of raw steak,
> he nibbled and guzzled, his jaw dripping weeds and bourbon.

These lines from "Love Fossil" refer to the father, the most prominent among Olds's cast of characters. Of the 531 poems in her nine collections to date, 107 deal in some way with the daughter's recollections of him. Most often, as the passage above illustrates, the father is rendered with comedic hostility. His depiction above goes beyond simply noting the Brobdingnagian proportions of a heavyset man or lamenting a childhood spent with an alcoholic patriarch—this is lyric character assassination. What is more, the evocation of a dinosaur (or unlikely chimera) is a grotesquerie unlike the slim, chipper patriarchs (think *Father Knows Best*) that hovered over the Eisenhower-era childhood setting for the poem. It is exactly this iconic representation of the nuclear family that confessional poetry, populated as it is with emotionally unavailable fathers and damaged households, stands against. As the poem progresses, this cumbersome beast slips into the tar pits and becomes a victim of his own intractable (but deserved?) extinction. Yet in the next line, the daughter expresses ironical and unexpected yearning: she describes the father as the "super sleazy extinct beast my heart dug for." It is this paradoxical description of a patriarch who is both ponderous and grotesque and an unattainable object of desire that fuels Olds's poems of fatherhood. Throughout her work Olds uses the daughter as a witness to the excesses of alcoholism, the American male, and the American milieu, particularly with respect to the representations of gender in 1950s suburbia. The portrait of the damaged patriarch and subverted family values is made all the more overt, all the more disturbing, and all the more telling as the daughter invokes her sexuality in her attempt to catch the father beast's herbivore gaze: "I flashed my animal sides, and he was / Vegetarian to the end."

As the second poem in Olds's first collection, *Satan Says,* "Love Fossil" must be given some prominence in her oeuvre. It is, more or less, an explication of the overarching narrative that has played out across Olds's nine volumes of poetry to date. The poem establishes the character of the man and also the character of the daughter's obsession. Sexuality is central, particularly when related to family history. Not surprisingly descriptions of the father are contradictory, as when he becomes spiritual, even godlike in Olds's seminal elegy *The Father.* But the standard image of the father is of an unrepentant man swallowed by his own demons, and the standard image of the daughter is as a frustrated adolescent both troubled and titillated by her father's remoteness. In these instances of sublimated incestuous desire, Olds inverts the notion of the male gaze and has made abjection desirable.

Theories of the male gaze revolve around the concept that observation changes the relationship between the observer and the observed and influences the way knowledge is generated. As specified in the theories of Laura Mulvey, the viewer attains a measure of power over the person or thing being viewed.[1] Mulvey postulates that in cinema, primarily male film directors use the camera to highlight the bodies of their actresses and titillate male viewers. Consequently female moviegoers are forced into watching sexualized versions of femininity as if they too were men observing a desirable object. This situation creates a triad of observation in which the gaze of the female audience is appropriated by the male perspective, including those women passively watching. Olds is an interesting poet in light of these theories: for her the gaze (particularly of the father and later the husband) is a sought-after enactment of male desire and thus attention. The daughter seeks empowerment through being seen rather than being the seer. Mulvey's theory is an argument against the objectification of a woman's body, but the daughter seems to desire just such objectification by the male gaze. Control for the daughter is a matter of being an object under observation.

The daughter responds to the degrading father's body as something to be embraced, and she longs for his gaze to fall upon her. Sexuality is wound into this need for the father's love, and somehow, in myriad images and statements of sublimated longing, this unrequited desire transfers itself to the daughter's own self-image. In "Love Fossil" she says of this dynamic that "he taught me to love / what was stuck, what couldn't help itself." At this early stage of the character's development, the daughter can only conceive of love as a slow-moving, slow-witted, self-defeated monster and herself as a ravening predator. "Carnivore that I was," she says, "I watched his / Bare white shoulder and I went hungry."

Thus early in Olds's career, the basic dicta for the father poems have been loosely established: the father is alcoholic, emotionally distant, self-destructive, chauvinistic, and apparently unaware of his effect upon his family; the daughter sublimates her frustration into disgust contradicted by longing, which is then shockingly manifested as sexual desire. Stylistically her anger expresses itself through surreal imagery and hyperbolic tropes, and this language has become a staple of Olds's art over the course of thirty-five years.

Additionally, despite the apparent seriousness of the father/daughter dynamic, "Love Fossil" also illustrates another aspect of Olds's poetics: she is very funny. It is gallows humor, to be sure, but the hyperbole lends itself to another literary theory, the notion of the comic grotesque, the blending of the funny and the horrible. Dark laughter often leads to healing, but it can also emphasize inappropriateness as a method of reducing behavior to its most radical, ridiculous components. The father, both unnatural monster and pathetic clown, embodies this mode of representation. The cannibal daughter who lusts after the meaty, bestial father is, in her own way, also a comic grotesque: she is ridiculous in her unwholesome desires to the point that her yearnings are exaggerated, even cartoonish.

Oddly enough, meat also signifies the father's anemic personality; it is a theme that Olds returns to only one other time, in "Aspic and Buttermilk" (*BTS* 18). In this poem the daughter exults that "my father himself could not eat liver—and I could eat liver." The depiction becomes even more antimasculine when she reveals that "he fainted at the sight / of a cut," particularly when "I could eat *raw* meat . . . the rubble of muscle / in my mouth." In this portrait the father is incapable of facing the more difficult situations in life, while the daughter is capable of chewing them whole. Dynamics of strength and ability are reversed between parent and child and even between traditional notions of gender. Nevertheless the father assumes a natural gendered superiority over women that manifests itself through boorish behavior, which is significant to Olds's overall dynamics of gender and family.

As example, in "His Costume" (*TUR* 24) the daughter recalls that, for costume parties, "my father liked to dress as a woman," which revealed his disdain for the gender: "He had his sign language about women / talking too much, and being stupid." This comic grotesque image of the transvestite patriarch apparently mincing, speaking in falsetto, and using his body language to mock openly the people whose visage he takes on—both literally in his apparel and implicitly in his assumption of male superiority—speaks to the character's hypocrisy and condescension. At the same time, however, the thing that makes him disagreeable also marks him as pathetic: he is unaware that he is humiliating himself and indicating the superiority of the gender he mocks. This is a paradox that Olds mines repeatedly in her poetry.

Note, for instance, in "My Father Snoring" (*TDATL* 41) that the daughter is both disgusted and fascinated by the grotesquerie of the father's cacophonous sleep, revealing her unlikely obsession with his physical self: she expresses revulsion but, often implicitly, finds herself in a version of physical intimacy symbolized by a kind of reverse intercourse. "I could feel myself inside his body," she says of the rhythm of the father's snoring, "lowered again, into the narrow / dark well, its amber walls / slick around my torso, the smell of bourbon / rich as sputum." Her need seems to be a connection with the father that she cannot get through normal avenues. In this pathology the naughty daughter must compensate for the lack of emotional connection with an imagined sexual union. Such sublimated desire is a reason why Olds's writing is dubbed sensational or pornographic by her detractors, and such descriptions deserve to be acknowledged, even as they miss the Freudian overtones of an Electra complex, a central them in Olds's poetry.

The emotions of Olds's characters, particularly the daughter, seem to exceed the situation. A prime example is in "History: 13" (*TGC* 26). In this poem the daughter finds her father drunk, unconscious, and bloodied on the living-room couch. Rather than inspiring a moment of filial empathy, the sight leads the daughter to compare her drunken father to the battered corpse of Benito Mussolini hung upside down from a meat hook by rioting partisans. Certainly the scenario, based as it is on the trauma of childhood memory, deserves a dramatic retelling, but the analogue to a deposed World War II dictator and the emphasis on the violence of his demise is extreme. Likewise in "The Victims" (*TDATL* 34), a recollection of her parents' divorce, the rest of the family "grinned inside, the way people grinned when / Nixon's helicopter lifted off." Two poems later, in "The Departure" (*TDATL* 36), which is dedicated "to my father," the daughter asks, "Did you weep like the Shah when you left?" Such emphasis on debauched and subsequently deposed world leaders leaves little room for hermeneutic uncertainty—the father is found guilty by his oppressed masses—yet the extremity of the comparisons verges on bathos when one considers the effect on American politics and culture of Watergate or the starvation and torture of Iranian people at the hands of the Shah. However, the father can also be read as a synecdoche of the major political movements shaping geopolitics on a microcosmic scale: the same dynamic of callous self-interest and absolute power found on the world's stage can also poison the middle-class household. To put this another way, the father is linked to major world events through the basic inhumanity common to all these bad men. And just as Richard Nixon and the Shah changed the course of international events, so too did the father change the course of his family's history.

The influence of the father perpetually shapes the consciousness of the female characters. In "Why My Mother Made Me" (TGC 33), the daughter wonders, "Maybe I am what she always wanted, I my father as a woman." The father appears in her imagination surrounded by "the hard male light of 1937," an image meant to sum up the ideal of rugged masculinity associated, at least in the daughter's mind, with the late 1930s. He is a prototypical male standing opposite the prototypical female of the era, and the gender roles implied by this pairing will provide fodder for their character portrayals throughout Olds's poetry. Olds's response, at least textually, is as a rebel with a cause; the ending image of "Why My Mother Made Me" is a sword that reflects the father's "face in the / steel of the blade." Once again the daughter battles the influences of the masculine and feminine in her life at precisely the time that the battle of the sexes was being waged in world culture. As such, she represents the individual's seeking identity and finding it in images of strength. Such a concept conflicts, among many conflicts in the poetry, with the daughter's own reaction to the father.

A longstanding convention in confessional poetry, which the daughter seems to reify, is Carl Jung's concept of the Electra complex. At its simplest the complex is the female counterpart to Sigmund Freud's Oedipus complex. A female child's development includes love for her father that is manifested, in part, by jealousy toward the mother. In Sophocles's play from which the name is taken, Electra and her brother, Orestes, avenge the murder of their father, Agamemnon, by killing their mother, Clytemnestra, and stepfather, Aegisthus. In psychoanalytic theory the revenge is the symbolic killing of the opposite-gendered parent (Jung designates the move as "jealousy") in the psyche and the identification with the same-gendered parent, thus rendering the child, now an adolescent, as sexually mature by sundering the dependence on the opposite-gendered parent. Healthy sexual development requires, in both Freud's and Jung's theories, that this murderous psychosexual process take place. It could be said that the confessional writers are Electra's offspring, constantly failing this private evolution and battling the influence of their fathers. Sylvia Plath said in a BBC interview about her "Daddy" that it is "a poem about a girl with an Electra complex."[2] Plath's father, who died when she was eight, is more overtly elegized in "Electra on Azalea Path," a somewhat surreal monologue the poet wrote about visiting her father's gravesite. In the poem mourning amounts to rejection and obsession and then to guilt: "I brought my love to bear," the speaker in the poem says, "and then you died." Actually one may read any of the confessional poets and find this same fascination with death and fatherhood. It should be apparent to anyone reading Olds's collections that she too follows this construct.

A complicated enactment of the Electra complex is narrated in "The Bed" (*BTS* 61), also a story of first encounters, in this case between the daughter and her stepmother. While the initial summit between these two could be more fraught, this is still a moment in which the daughter's childhood pathology is given new impetus. The poem begins as the new wife gazes earnestly, nervously, "looking out a window," apparently waiting for the daughter to arrive home from school. The new wife, her "hands in the suds," is involved in a very traditional mother role. Olds provides here one of the few descriptions of the daughter that is not masked in metaphoric construction: readers are told that the new wife "saw a tall, dark-haired teenager / turn the corner." Such details are not unique or terribly revealing, but they do hint at a certain awkward coltishness in the daughter and paint a blurry picture of someone much like Olds herself. In a few moments, the elder woman (possessed of knowledge, carnal and otherwise) will come into contact with an adolescent who is seeking such knowledge. "I gazed at her—," the daughter says; "this was the woman my father loved. / My father was in love!" The young woman is dealing with a new, startling concept now that the original family constellation has been destroyed; the encoded dyadic structure formed in the child's mind by the mother and father no longer exists and, instead, the mother has been replaced by a stranger. Despite or perhaps because of this dynamic, the new wife and the daughter find themselves enacting a ritual of hearth and home: the new stepmother fixes the stepdaughter a meal. It is very simply stated in the poem—"She fed me something, / I ate and beheld until we heard his key / in the lock." The father finds them "standing together, flushed, blushing—." Narration moves quickly here, efficiently. In this instance Olds simply says what needs to be said.

Again, as with a great deal of Olds's oeuvre, particularly those instances dealing with the father/daughter relationship, the narrative takes the unavoidable swerve to sex. "He pushed / a button—and down, out of the wall, fell / a double bed . . . Their Murphy / bed of love!"

Once one examines the scenario, the comic surprise is perfectly natural under the circumstances and as awkward as wedding night jitters. The sudden appearance of the Murphy bed symbolizes the realization of the father's sexuality and allows the daughter to imagine a level of superiority to the new wife based entirely upon the diminution of the sexual act.

After that,
when I thought of them, I thought of their bed
snapping shut, like a mouse trap,
holding them pressed there, against the wall,
in violent climax, crushed together.

This should be enough, one could argue, to seal the psychological boundaries for the daughter, but Olds goes further and constructs a series of metaphors for sex: "the stamen indented into the pistil, / the anther bent over the petal." For all its apparent cruelty, Olds's humor is also apparent. The father's ham-handed attempt to lighten the mood is elevated into a satire of desire. It is no more ridiculous to imagine his penis as an anther (the part of the stamen that contains the pollen) than it is to imagine a slapstick calamity of the marriage bed.

Yet in a final reversal of emotions, the daughter conceives of the couple without the cruel sense of humor often on display in her narratives about the father:

the man
and woman as God had made them, almost
my parents, in love.

As is generally the case, the daughter does not entirely comprehend her emotions here, and much of her psychic dislocation comes out later when she deals with the father's death from cancer in *The Father.*

If there is an explanation for this extremity of emotion that seems to exceed the circumstances, it is the intensity of family relations. Olds evokes the worst figures and events of geopolitics in order to provide a correlative to the emotions of the private individual, no matter how excessive such a comparison might seem. A gloomy evening with a bloodied father snoring drunkenly on the living-room couch cannot realistically be compared to the experiences of World War II victims; yet to the private individual, such experiences loom large in the mind, particularly from the vantage of childhood. In the final evaluation, the family is serious business. One overriding concern in Olds's poetry is the effect that the family has on children and on further descendants.

"The Guild" (*TDATL* 17) traces the Father's psychology back to its source: the grandfather. A tableau poem, it describes a dark, fire-lit room that represents the psychological venue of the family. It repeats the refrain "Every night, as my grandfather sat / in the darkened room in front of the fire." Generally the hearth is associated with home, warmth, and comfort, yet here it evokes cold and fearsomeness. Images of darkness and fire symbolize the twin illnesses of rage and alcoholism that shape the characters of both the grandfather and the father; the latter, an "apprentice," sits next to the grandfather with his own "glass of coals" in his hand. The young father is portrayed with surprising delicacy as a "college boy with white skin, unlined, a narrow / beautiful face." As with many of Olds's poems of social commentary, people are victims of their circumstances, as if the narrator is examining the processes that shape her characters. At its deepest reading, "The Guild" is really about the daughter's understanding of the father. She comprehends the forces that shaped him, but she is unstinting in her anger toward him. Eventually the father will "pass his master in cruelty and oblivion," and this lineage of alcoholism and rage will be passed from father to daughter: in a later poem in *The Dead and the Living*, the daughter says, "I see I am / my father as a woman" ("Poem to My Husband from My Father's Daughter"). This is a motion begun early in her collections and carried forward throughout her work. "The Guild," like "I Go Back to May 1937," is the root poem in a sequence that explores the dynamic of family dysfunction, for which the father is the prime instigator and perennial symbol. In this instance and in many like it, Olds implies that environment is the basis of behavior, although this is a problematic, not entirely resolved issue in the poetry. At times the lineage of cruelty is a somewhat mysterious force, part environmental and part genetic. In another poem in *The Dead and the Living*, "The Eye" (referring to the grandfather's glass eye), the "bad grandfather wouldn't feed us," would turn out the lights as the children tried to read, and then would sit alone, drinking "in front of the hearth." As is often the case, the daughter turns her focus onto herself and questions about her own character. She wonders

> how I am
> one-fourth him, a brutal man with a
> hole for an eye, and one-fourth her,
> a woman who protected no one.

This notion—of the woman intimidated into silence by men—has resonances throughout Olds's poetry, most overtly in "Sunday Night" (*TUR* 14), when "my father would put his hand up a waitress's / skirt if he could" and the daughter regrets that "I never warned her." It is a somewhat ironic notion, considering that the speaker is a woman who, while obviously not silenced, still carries psychological scars from these emotionally brutal men.

In "The Sign of Saturn" (*TDATL* 73), this mysterious dynamic of lineage is transferred to the daughter's own progeny:

> Sometimes my daughter looks at me with an
> amber black look, like my father
> about to pass out from disgust.

Olds's theme is the influence of family on children. Her emphasis, which she sustains throughout her work, is to escape this world, both as a woman overcoming the hegemony of men and as a parent passing this triumph onto her children. The father and grandfather stand as the prime exemplars of what *not* to be, as both men and parents.

A further paradox of the father, given all of the above, comes in the form of the conceits used to portray him: while many of Olds's earliest poems describe him as a comic grotesque or worse, in later poems he is often described in terms of a cosmic event or a deity. However, as with his initial portrayal in "Love Fossil," these evocations are seldom flattering. A prime example is "Saturn" (*TGC* 24), in which the inebriated patriarch is depicted as a black hole literally pulling the light from the environment—"He lay on the couch night after night, / mouth open, the darkness of the room / filling his mouth"—and then evolves into the cannibalistic, infanticidal figure of myth evoked in the title:

> My brother's arm went in up to the shoulder
> and he bit it off, and sucked the wound,
> as one sucks at the sockets of the lobster.

This allusion is to the nightmarish *Saturn Devouring His Son* (1823) by Francisco Goya. The grotesquerie and violence of in the painting lend themselves well to Olds's sense of melodrama and hyperbole. And the myth likewise lends itself to Olds's theme of fatherhood and its potential for psychic damage; Saturn castrates his father, Ouranos (the sky), in a royal coup that, despite its gruesome success, results in his intense paranoia about his own children. Important to this discussion are the conjoined images of the father and god figures. "Saturn" is one of Olds's many childhood memory poems that utilizes descriptors and allusions to represent the father as a powerful and terrible deity. "Saturn" is an important poem that has resonances in all of Olds's collections, and she has returned to this scene repeatedly throughout her poetry.

In other instances, however, Olds humanizes the father by rendering him as either maternal or as weak and vulnerable. The change is physical as well as spiritual. His masculine persona undergoes either an evolution into the maternal, in which case he is portrayed affectionately, or a devolution into abjection, where he becomes an object of desire. "My Father's Breasts" (*TDATL* 43) is one of the former, in which the father evolves into a feminized and thus more palatable version of himself. As with many of her family poems, "My Father's Breasts" is a memory poem predicated upon a simple scenario: the daughter as a little girl snuggles in the father's lap and places her ear upon his chest. This experience and its accompanying sensations are then endowed with complex imagery that could be read as cultural, spiritual, and even earthly. At this moment of physical intimacy, the father takes on the physical attributes traditionally (or conservatively) associated with women—gentleness, softness, comfort—through the ritual of holding a child. Any implications of the father as sexualized are forgone. Rather, he is rendered in language that implies a tempered and feminized physical manifestation of his otherwise callous persona: the hair on his chest is "polished silk . . . running down the man-breasts" of middle age "delicately / like water." The daughter remembers hearing "the black / charge of the heart within," perhaps for the only time. As in a number of the father poems, he is connected with exterior light and interior darkness. It is as if the father—*this* father—is an object with a hard, elegant surface that closes off a lightless interior.

Nevertheless, by the end of the poem, the daughter imagines herself cuddling for years against the father she so vehemently denounces elsewhere. And the final sensation, the "smell of black pepper and / turned earth," is a surprisingly homey, pleasant, even healthy association with organic and romantic nature. At the same time, however, these final allusions are vaguely unsettling—the scent of pepper is pungent and perhaps even painful, while "turned earth" could refer to the work of the plow, and thus renewal and growth, but also carries implications of burial and the grave. Such abstraction speaks to the daughter's own ambivalence about the father and her inability to resolve the issues explored in other poems. In this unusual portrait of the father—surprisingly empathetic if overall disquieting—Olds exposes her characters' latent familial affection. However, such moments of humanization and change are incongruous with the father's previous incarnations, unless Olds revises the trope of the father's body (which throughout has served as synecdoche for dominant male culture) as an implicit call to action. It is instances such as these in which Olds's artistry as a protest poet is most prominent.

Another iteration of this theme occurs when the father is devolved into abjection through humiliation and thus rendered more vulnerable and sympathetic. "Once" (*BTS* 21) is a strangely comfortable poem about a typical embarrassment of family life:

> I saw my father naked, once, I
> opened the blue bathroom door

. . . .
and there, surround by glistening turquoise
tile, sitting on the toilet, was my father.

The daughter instinctively observes the father's body "in a single, swerving, unimpeded / swoop" and perceives it as "so seamless, and shy, like a girl on a toilet." And then she apologetically retreats—a natural course of events. Such an experience is commonplace, and such a frank revelation as this can be read as an unflinching, even tender discussion of the humanity all people share at the biological level. In fact the daughter recalls that

even though I knew he was sitting
to shit, there was no shame in that
but even a human peace.

At the same time, Olds is unafraid to make an implication about sexuality and incestuous desire:

. . . I'd seen him, my father a shorn lamb,
my father a cloud in the blue sky
of the blue bathroom, my eye had driven
up the hairpin mountain road of the
naked male.

At this point one is tempted to question whether or not Olds has found a convenient commercial niche—issues of the comic grotesque aside, she seems to revel in the embarrassing aspects of American life everyone knows about but prefers not to examine. Honesty, common sense might dictate, has its bounds. Arguably in this context, Olds's poetry is predicated upon deliberate transgression, particularly of middle-class decorum. And the merit of such candid humanizing of an otherwise unlikable character is debatable, particularly when the portrait is by its nature unlikable.

Conversely "The Ideal Father" (*TDATL* 38), as its title implies, reflects the daughter's own intense need for a positive father figure; she imagines, down to the minutest detail, the physical attributes of the perfect patriarch. Skin, fat, teeth, hair, nipples, even the phallus are considered. Olds again utilizes a surreal diction of the unhindered imagination, flush with its gratuitous yoking of image and metaphor—subcutaneous fat, for instance, is "pearls"; the "necks and roots" of the perfect teeth are likened to "squids' legs, deep in the gum"; and nipples are "pink carnation *boutonnieres*." Such detail identifies human perfection specifically in the province of the body, and in the construction of the poem, this visceral focus has a pointed rhetorical tactic in the last complex sentence of the poem: "After all," the daughter says of this imagined exemplar, "he has daughters to protect, laying his perfect / body over their sleep all night long." Such a longing harks back to childhood and the idealized security of the bedroom with the light of the parents' bedroom door just down the hall.

Yet despite all that readers know of the man, in the poem that follows "The Ideal Father," aptly titled "Fate" (*TDATL* 40), the daughter returns to the notion that temperament is a matter of heritage; she says baldly, "Finally I just gave up and became my father." And in this instance she catalogs the physical failures of the nonidealized, dystopic father figure, his "defeated face," "mud brown eyes . . . glistening like wet ground," "bad breath," "slumped posture of failure," and, expectedly, "his sad / sex dangling on his thigh" below "his stomach swollen and empty." The disheveled and frankly disgusting father is meant as a point-by-point rebuke to the imagined ideal father only a poem before. It is, as implied in the title, pure "fate" that the daughter will become the father.

As Olds's career has progressed, however, the focus on the father has gradually faded away. Poetry about children, politics, and the mother has taken center stage. In "Directly" (*TUR* 54) the daughter acknowledges the healing nature of time. "Then, one late afternoon," she says, "I understand: the harm my father / did us is receding." She records a moment of clarity: "But he had not been hated, so he did not hate us, / just scorned us, and it is wearing off." She recognizes that her own children are inexplicably free of the lineage of psychic damage—"they are well / as if by some miracle"—and she conceives of them as animal spirits facing the symbolic direction of natural death, "the starlings all facing / the west, his grave." The genealogical cycle of abuse has been broken. And the daughter finally distinguishes her own need for closure and visits the grave of the patriarch; it is an ambiguous ending in which the father's grave is "home" and his "done-with body" is "broken back down into earth" yet still holds "its solemn incapable beauty." The visceral degradation first dramatized in "Love Fossil" has reached a qualified resolution in the dignity of death.

The Father

Olds's landmark *The Father* (1997) is a book-length elegy about the death of the titular character from throat cancer. The collection consists of fifty-two poems, which together create a narrative spanning approximately three years, in which the father is portrayed with a surprising reverence. Soon after the actual death, however, the daughter's sorrow turns into rage and a sense of abandonment. As if to reflect these competing emotions, Olds creates a distinct double motion in the book, contrasting the disintegration of the father's physical body with the elevation of his spirit; as he dies he begins to shine and to take on the attributes of a god. While the poems themselves run continuously, the plotline of the collection is divided into five sections, almost as if the book follows the five-act structure of drama. These sections roughly constitute the first act, which could also be considered a prologue (the first three poems before the father is hospitalized); a second act in the hospital as he begins to fail (nineteen poems, from "The Glass" to "Psalm"); a third act that describes the actual death (seven poems, from "My Father's Eyes" to "The Feelings"); a fourth, longest, and most complicated act composed of sentimentalized recollections (fifteen poems, from "After Death" to "The Pull"); and the final fifth act, which returns to the theme of the destructive father (the remaining seven poems). By the end of the collection, the daughter comes to a catharsis, but it is a qualified resolution that will work itself out itinerantly through the rest of her oeuvre.

In those poems that humanize the man, the father's decline is often accompanied, again paradoxically, by aristocratic and deific conceits. Images of monarchy, fire, and celestial bodies predominate. For instance in "The Lumens" (11), a title that refers both to a standard measurement of light and to small lighting instruments used by nurses, the father literally emits light from his dying self:

> sluices of shining come out of his eyes.
> It is frightening to see how much light
> this night man has had in him.

Objects and other characters are suffused with light when they come in contact with the father in a series of complex, alternating symbols. In "The Present Moment" (20) the old father of darkness and drunkenness is forgotten, and instead he is compared to "a Channel swimmer" whose "limbs / glow, faintly, in the night water." Likewise the same man who could not eat "dense, earthen food, like liver" because he was unable to chew on the metaphoric pith of life now eats "things like pineapple, wedges of light, the skeiny nature of light made visible." Essentially the daughter has come to a moment of reconciliation now that the patriarch is dying, and her emotion is expressed metaphorically. At its simplest such instances exhibit a version of the pathetic fallacy in which the exterior world manifests the emotional state of the narrator. On a more complex reading, Olds utilizes the archetypal symbol of light to summon any number of familiar associations (life, afterlife, birth, rebirth, illumination, knowledge, even a measure of newfound purity or the presence of a deity)—many meanings can be attributed to this particular image in the poetry. These are largely affirmative in *The Father.*

Primarily, however, light symbolizes the father's vital force now muted by the sheen of death, and it also reifies the emotional strain upon the daughter as she perceives this shadow. This in turn creates two paradoxes: first that the weakening human body can exert such a blinding grip on the psyche, and second that tropes that represent the father become sublime at the moments when his death is most apparent. Throughout the collection the daughter registers increasing shock and mourning, as would be expected, and this generates a clairvoyance of hindsight. Light infuses the daughter's memory—because the entire collection is based on memory, as any elegy would be—whenever recollection becomes overwrought. These images are emblematic of the collective consciousness of the father's family and hospice workers and his relationship to the unseen world. Such is the power of a parent over a child: the father shines as if he were an elemental force in the world, literally with the same power as the sun or moon. In fact much of the narrative thrust of the collection is the attempt to come to grips with these moments where the father appears to be an object of supernatural influence. Also it should be remembered that fire symbolizes the destructive mental illness of the family patriarchs. As life wanes in the essential father figure, *fire* transforms in the expressionistic lens of the daughter into symbols and metaphors of sublimated love. This is not to suggest, however, that *The Father* is an elegy in the traditional sense of a plaintive but affectionate portrait. Rather it moves through the prelude to death, to the emotional turbulence of the death itself, to the immediate grief afterward, and to open resentment as the final aftermath.

The first three poems of *The Father* establish the conflicting nature of the daughter's experience. In "The Waiting" (3), for instance, the father is objectified as a "sculpture." The daughter says that "he had / a way of holding still to be looked at." The theme of father as object occurs only once more in the collection, in "The Want" (14), the tenth poem, when the daughter says, "I had / always known him as an object in the world / of objects because he would not speak." In this evocation the father is both an idealized representation and self-aware living art, the character's cold self-absorption and destructive charisma manifest.

In the second poem, "Nullipara" (5) (a designation for a woman who has never given birth), and the third poem, "The Pulling" (6), the daughter establishes two additional contradictory emotional themes. In "Nullipara" she recognizes that the father will "live in" her after his death and that she will "carry him like a mother"; nevertheless the toxic family history will hamper the process of psychological gestation: "I do not know if I will ever deliver." On the other hand, in "The Pulling" the daughter says, "I sense every inch of him moving / through me . . . the way each child / moved, slowly, down through my body." She equates this motion to God, rivers, even the universe coursing through her "as if," she concludes, "my father could live and die / safely inside me." Such contradictions speak to the daughter's own conflicted emotions concerning her father and her own renewal through motherhood.

The fourth poem, "The Glass" (7), is one of Olds's best-known and most important poems. The unlikely subject is a hospital drinking glass filled with the mucus discharge from the tumor in the father's throat. Instead of revulsion the glass represents the grand forces of the universe and the daughter's devotion to her father. Time and distance provide the daughter with a lens to examine this most painful memory, and her examination provides her with the incongruous trope of solar fire to describe sickening bodily discharge; the outlandishness of this combination is offset by the seriousness of the situation, almost as if the narrator wishes to relegate the memory to the realm of the supernatural to distance herself from it. At the heart of this juxtaposition is the terrible, fantastic destructive power of the father's body and the daughter's need to sublimate this realization into extraordinary imagery. The equation of bodily discharge with solar flares in turn leads to free association of a rather surreal image of "pouring tongues," an uncomfortably literal description of the tumor's extrusions.

What justifies this extraordinary tropology is the effect of her father's cancer upon the narrator: for her the illness is an event that alters reality; the universe will never be the same, the physics of personality have changed. Even the power of the stars or the eruption of Vesuvius can hold hardly more emotional value for the daughter, who looked up from her childhood crib to see the wonder of her father looming overhead. Thus it is imagery of the sun, the power source of terrestrial life, that also signals the terrible reality of her father's imminent death. Like an apocalyptic visionary, the daughter fights a losing battle against the inexorable march of death by generating images that match the grand design of her universe, and this once again relates to terrible biology. The rest of the poem is replete with the physical details of the illness, the "gargle, cough, spit," the hacking, the "scraping the rim of his lower lip to / get the last bit off his skin" that consume the dying man's last breaths. All the while the glass "sits there . . . shiny and faintly golden" like the father's grail.

Yet in line 18, the father "is like a god producing food from his own mouth." Once again wonder is combined with horror, the grotesque with the miraculous. The glass itself has many resonances in the scenario: an emblem of both the physical horror of death and the fantastic nature of bodily processes even while it serves as a reminder of the artificiality of the environment. In the same moment, the glass is a talisman of the father's psychological power, which seems to amplify as the physical body deteriorates. The poem then returns to an unflinching look at physical illness: the father is once again a grotesquerie consumed by the hunger of the tumor.

The portrayal is an alternative to the motif of father as divinity seen throughout the book, and the fact of the glass's existence must be tended to lest it create mess and contagion in this sterile, artificial world. From here the father simply weakens, and the imagery is distinctly visceral, personal, and detailed. Clearly the daughter is fulfilling her role as the good child, and her ability to deal with the terrible physicality of the situation with this level of objectivity is possible only because of the human ability to postpone trauma. The argument could be made that post-traumatic stress—the constant reliving of traumatic situations, the inability of the mind to process intense fear, the reordering of experience—provides a rubric for the tropology found in *The Father,* and this aspect of trauma accounts for the intensity of the experience in the daughter's memory. As the daughter watches, the glass begins to

> shimmer there on the table until the
> room seemed to turn around it
> in an orderly way, a model of the solar system
> turning around the gold sun,
> my father the dark earth that used to
> lie at the center of the universe.

The father is now the rich soil of the birth planet, yet even his own gravity is not enough to remain the contact point, and the glass, representing death, is now the center of the universe before which the characters stand mute and abject.

"The Glass" also has interesting implications for the elegy. The poem provides an odd and terrible portrait of the subject, an expression of love and loss (albeit buried symbolism), truly metaphysical sadness (also wound into the symbol of the glass), and consolation (implied through the fantastic solar metaphors). Yet again the persona of the father is one of weird disgust, which follows the persona established early in Olds's canon. If there are issues of fate and justice involved, the father has achieved a measure of greatness through the act of dying itself.

However in the following poem, "Death and Morality" (9), the daughter says, "My father's dying is not evil. / It is not good and it is not evil, / it is out of the moral world altogether." The father has entered a world of "no guilt, no shame," only "pleasure and pain." Reduced to pure physical sensation, the father once again has the status of revered object. Nevertheless the companion poems "His Terror" (12) and "His Stillness" (13) dramatize the unavoidable fear of death and yet grant the father unusual dignity. He is seen in the company of a priest—an extremely unusual scenario—who he calls, tellingly, *father*—as he receives Communion from this religious patriarch. At this point the daughter wonders about her father's fear of death and concludes, "Maybe his terror is not of dying . . . but of some cry / he has kept inside him all his life." Once again the theme of the unfulfilled man emerges, yet why the father experiences such agony is not revealed in the poetry. "His Stillness," however, provides a portrait that is antithetical to all previous pictures of the father. Learning that his condition is terminal, the Father responds surprisingly "with the dignity of a foreign leader." And the daughter's response is equally surprising: "At the / end of his life his life began / to wake in me."

This complex function of the father, particularly as it relates to the concept of an imago, is most apparent in "Wonder" (25). Olds here reifies the power of the parent from the child's point of view. As with many of the poems in *The Father,* "Wonder" is composed of snapshots of memory stacked as if on an album page. It takes place in the hospital as the daughter goes to the father's death watch. At this point of heightened emotional strain, what reveals itself suddenly to the daughter is a memory out of childhood:

> The planet of his head
> swam above my crib, I did not understand it.
> His body came toward me in the lake over the agates,
> the hair of his chest lifting like root-hairs—
> I saw it and I did not understand it.

It is a moment in which one character becomes the perceiving subject and the other becomes an object of such magnitude that it is beyond explanation. This is a moment of sublime identification: the *wonder* of that moment when her father's head swam above the crib remains tantamount, even as an adult going to meet her father's withered shell; even when his most salient moments in her life are relegated to memory, the father is a sublime object, ultimately comparable to the earth itself, or a god, or a cosmic event. Father as god is a recurring theme throughout the collection. In "My Father's Eyes" (31), the daughter watches the father's delirium manifest as a series of vague eye movements, which she likens to an apocalyptic vision: "if God had blinked, / a world unmade in the jump of an eyelid." As in "The Glass," the symptoms of the father's illness take on the force of the universe, because for the daughter the universe is sundering. In such descriptions there exists (arguably) a fair amount of filial devotion sublimated into distancing images of surrealism, and yet from the death scene in the hospital forward, the emotional palate slowly begins to turn toward familiar expressions of the Electra complex.

The turning point actually occurs midway through the third, reflective section of *The Father* with paired poems, "Beyond Harm" (52) and "The Underlife" (53). These two poems illustrate the alternating tides of love and hate in the daughter's psyche. "Beyond Harm" begins in recollection, a week after the father's death, as the daughter realizes that "his fondness for me was safe—nothing / could touch it." Now, postmortem, memories of the man can be manipulated. "He respected my spunk," the daughter asserts, returning to a common plaint; "when they tied me to the chair, that time, / they were tying up someone he respected." Even during his bouts of self-imposed silence (the only reference to this behavior in the poetry), the daughter reasons, "I was one of the / beings to whom he was not speaking, / someone with a place in his life." Such resolutions are, perhaps, too easily achieved and their resonances too easily accepted. Then in "The Underlife" this dynamic explodes, and sublimation gives way to more expected expressions of rage and disgust. Waiting for a subway, "looking down / into the pit where the train rides," the daughter spies a rat and then a cockroach—two vermin associated with underground New York—and these suddenly transform into avatars of the "bourbon and then the cancer" that pulled the father under. The vision becomes distinctly nightmarish as the daughter reconnects to the dark underbelly of her psychology:

> roach and rat turn to me
> with that swiveling turn of natural animals, and they
> say to me We are not educators,
> we come to you from him.

From this point on in the collection, the connotations in the poems vacillate between unquenchable longing ("The Pull," 65) and frustrated ire ("Letter to My Father from 40,000 Feet," 63), sometimes combining the two ("Natural History" and "The Cigars"). The father is imagined as Charon, the boatman over the river Styx, in "The Ferryer" (67), a poem ostensibly about his darkling character but really about the daughter's own relational scars:

> When I dump someone in
> he does not look back, he takes them straight
> to hell. He wants to work for me
> until I die.

This is an allegory. The dead represent loss—emotional, familial, romantic, sexual—and the ferryman (the father) pilots the vehicle of this loss; he is the captain of the daughter's psychological vessel, and by the end of the poem the daughter predicts her own crossing: she will "get in his boat" and ride to the opposite shore, where the antagonistic duo will "embrace like two who were never born" and "rest together at the end of the working day." The daughter is an analogue for either Dido or Odysseus, depending on how one reads the poem, descending to the underworld to speak to her dead progenitor about the future. It is a fatalistic vision replete with expected melodrama and tragic denouement.

For the first time, the father character speaks. "When the Dead Ask My Father about Me" (73) is a dramatic monologue in which, apparently guilty, the father admits to absolute failures in life yet appears to venerate the jury. The central conceit of dirt—stopping the father's mouth and surrounding his body—aligns with the silence of death, a muteness that staunched him even in life. "No, I could not speak about" his daughter, he begins. "This dirt, I have always had it in my mouth." Surprisingly, however, the father reveals affection for his "second daughter" and her problematic personality and passions. He alludes vaguely to his disastrous first marriage; to lying in an alcoholic stupor, the tableau described in "Saturn"; and to the daughter's personification of frankly incestuous desires: "I loved / to pick up the foot of her bed, while she slept, / and drop it. / She was a dream to tease." Then the dialogue turns to the limited geography of the father's life ("I was only in New York once"), which allegorizes the limits of his accomplishments when compared to the daughter's ("when she moved to New York / she went to the Mayor's house for lunch, to / Gracie mansion, on business"). But his most significant statement, one that is perhaps self-serving on behalf of the daughter, is to see his progeny as his spokeswoman: "She could / speak, you see. As if my own / jaws, throat, and larynx had come / alive in her." However it is unclear if the daughter is receptive to this gift. "But," he says, "all she wanted / was that dirt from my tongue," and in the final turn, the father says, "I am audible, listen! this is *my* song." Olds seems to judge both her characters in this evaluation—the stagnation of the father versus the obstinate rage of the daughter.

Two poems later, in "Waste Sonata" (76), she says simply, "I knew. I saw him and judged him." As the daughter returns to the scene in "Saturn," however, she finally comes to a painful reckoning:

> I stood
> in that living room and saw him drowse
> like the prince, in slobbrous beauty I began
> to think he was a kind of chalice,
> a grail, his love the goal of a quest,
> yes! He was the god of love
> and I was a shit.

The poem turns thematically into an ars poetica—as if the daughter is repeatedly evaluating her own obsessions—when she says, "I love the terms of foulness. I have learned / to get pleasure of speaking of pain." Ultimately "Waste

Sonata" uses abjection to describe the family as "shits that move through him . . . waste foetuses," as a conceit for the ultimate effect of patriarchal abuse.

So it is not particularly surprising when *The Father* culminates in decay and debris to sum up the father's persona, an array of images Olds reuses in later iterations of the character. "My Father Speaks to Me from the Dead" (78) codifies the daughter's final analysis of the man. It is also the second poem in which he speaks directly to the reader. Peter C. Scheponik, in his reading of the poem, argues that "Sharon Olds resurrects her father to extract the emotional validation from him that she never received when he was alive"; this longing pits "her father's philosophy of the physical against her own emotional needs" and results in "an intense struggle for love and affirmation that ends in loss and rejection."[3] A great deal of Olds's poetry deals with this dynamic. In "My Father Speaks," the titular narrator is finally forced to confront the emotional combat, and—while there is no clean resolution (and thus "loss and rejection" remain unhealed)—the father actually confesses his qualified love for his child in terms that are implicitly sexualized.

In his final performance, the father wakes, slightly disoriented, on an unlikely stage, a "pot-shed . . . the bright paths / of slugs kiss-crossing my body." Scheponik focuses on the implications of the scene and their symbolic correlations to the father's life and character: the clay of the shed (too hard for vegetative growth), the shards of pots (which cannot hold life), and "the spider glue-net" (which plugs the father's mouth). "These opening images establish an alienated, flawed physical state," Scheponik has written, "offering little hope of comfort or love."[4] As if to confirm a "philosophy of the physical," the father's dialogue focuses on his daughter's body, at first distancing himself from the unavoidable sexual tension between them and then, on closer examination, admitting to having knowledge of her body but preferring to couch this admission in the safety of abstraction ("I love your—what can I call it, / between your legs"). The father reluctantly adumbrates fatherly intimacy through a series of uncomfortable observations about the daughter's body that do not, on the surface, sound fatherly. He performs the kind of scrutiny usually reserved for lovers. He loves her legs, buttocks, navel, breasts, and mind—and yet, as disturbing as this seems, it is clear from his monologue that these expressions have to do with child rearing: her legs are "your our my legs . . . yours and mine both," because he helped create her; her "tiny bottom" reminds him of changing her as a baby and how in that physical act of intimacy he "crossed wires with God"; and her breasts inspire a vision of his grandchild nursing while his spirit gazes out from the infant's eyes at the daughter who is the link between the generations. His only truly unaccountable analogy is the likening of her brain to "a woman's labia." Even this, however, can be read as his recognition of the primal difference between genders—what he found so difficult to say in life—which will always inhibit true visceral intimacy. Interestingly "My Father Speaks" is the poem in which the father says "I love your" a total of eleven times. Nevertheless in the final volte-face, he admonishes the daughter to look to her own power of expression for validation: he tells her to "look down at your hand," which has the ability to write, and "move it" in the act of writing, because "that action is matter's love"—the love of the earth. He also warns her that "for human / love" she should "go elsewhere." Scheponik's thesis is apt: the void between the physical world of matter and love is too great to be bridged, and the daughter's deep desire for the father's attention will never be fulfilled despite his badly expressed love.

Conclusion

Even in *The Wellspring,* putatively dedicated to the mother—and a counterpoint of sorts to Olds's Electra complex—the father still holds psychological real estate. In "The Swimming Race" (16), Olds once again returns to memories of childhood and the role of fatherhood. The poem is a brief narrative about a race in the Orinda Park Pool, a private swim club in Orinda, California, in which the juvenile daughter dog paddles to last place in front of a crowd that includes her new nemesis, the sister.

> I had surfaced, and started to dog-paddle, they had
> finished the race, their fathers had drawn them up
> dripping and were handing them sateen ribbons with rosettes,
>   a red and cobalt blue.

The character of the father to this point has been the disassociated lout and psychic brute of "Love Fossil," but suddenly here—as if consolation in an elegy—the daughter learns the value of perseverance and dignity from the same man who drunkenly cannibalized her siblings.

> I held my head as he'd taught me, and swam
> like a dog toward the end of the pool.

She has a moment factoring the danger of water, observing the "black lines / on the bottom of the pool, where the drowned would lie," but then from this alien vision the daughter looks up and sees at the end of the swimming lane the father. He exudes comfort and power and holds forth a typical childhood motivator and reward: candy.

> I paddled, I felt myself approach him,
> I was grinning because of the prize I would win

> For coming in third, a Big Hunk bar—
> the milk and honey on the other side—
> and because my father was getting bigger,
> leaning toward me, his arms open.

Olds is careful about her choice of pop culture, and a Big Hunk carries with it the double entendre of the "hunk" father, the big man who is both attractive and heroic. It is a rare occasion, in a lifetime spent befouling the role of patriarch, on which the father fulfills his obligation as protector and rational adult.

> He pulled me out, and held my hand
> up by the wrist. My sister sneered, she said
> *Why did you lift Shary's fist*
> *when she was last?* and he smiled, a smile almost
> without meanness, one of the last
> times we saw him smile, he said
> I thought she was the winner of the next race.

The daughter has been rescued on several fronts here: she is lifted from the literal danger she only dimly, almost dreamily realizes and into the safe arms of the parent; she is reassured, as a child should be, of her own small victory; and the father's superiority over his creation acts as a protective shield against the kind of psychic violence children, particularly siblings, are happy to mete upon each other.

On other occasions as the daughter heals, grows, and gazes backward on her obsession, Olds can have a more empathetic approach to her favorite subject. Originally published in *Poetry* in 1998 and then in *Blood, Tin, Straw,* "My Father's Diary" (69) is one of the few father poems in which the father has a voice of sorts. As the title suggests, the narrator has found the father's diary and reads a few key passages—those dealing with his young romance with the mother—for the readers as a form of portraiture that is both critical but strangely sympathetic toward him. As with so many of the father poems, the daughter begins the narration with a somewhat disquieting allusion to the Electra complex—"I get into bed with it, and spring / the scarab legs of its lock"—but then the narration turns to the "stacked, shy wealth of his print": she peers into the mind and character of the father with the sort of unfettered access that a diary, with its revelation of private moments, can bestow. What she finds is a simple hand, simple thoughts, and an inability to express himself. Nevertheless this lack of aptitude is counterbalanced by a hopeful, boyish vitality. The father "could not write in script," the daughter observes, and this lack of finesse, which will later turn to brutishness, is treated elegiacally. And yet "the pages / are sturdy with the beamwork of printedness." He has written exclusively in upper case, perhaps signifying, in addition to childlike simplicity, the sheer masculinity of the diary's author:

> WENT TO LOOK AT A CAR, DAD
> IN A GOOD MOOD AT DINNER, WENT
> TO TRY OUT SOME NEW TENNIS RACQUETS,
> LUNCH WITH MOM.

To which the daughter adds "life of ease—." It is an elegiac moment, the portrait of the man written in stark but bold strokes. The reader is meant to understand that these are the salad days, the halcyon moments of his life; Olds's readership knows what comes next—the abuse, the alcoholism, the dysfunction, the visceral disgust. But at this moment the simple pleasures in life are enough to fill his pages. He is a tremendously unimaginative young man, and the daughter fills in the creative gaps and describes how "a young tree whirled up to the / hood, throwing up her arms" when the father wrecked the grandfather's DeSoto. What sounds like a typical American rite of passage—the wrecking of the old man's car—can actually be read as an omen, because in the next turn of the poem, the mother enters the narrative as a kind of impossible adolescent dream:

> LOIS. PLAYED TENNIS, WITH LOIS,
> LUNCH WITH MOM AND LOIS, LOIS
> LIKED THE CAR, DRIVING WITH LOIS,
> LONG DRIVE WITH LOIS. And then,
> LOIS! I CAN'T BELIEVE IT! SHE IS SO
> GOOD, SO SWEET, SO GENEROUS, I HAVE
> NEVER, WHAT HAVE I EVER DONE
> TO DESERVE SUCH A GIRL?

The name "Lois" is invoked seven times in the father's diary. She is the only character other than the daughter whose actual name is given in Olds's poems about her family. The father is suffering a clear case of puppy love, though Olds's readers again know what the future brings for everyone involved. Rather than delving into this sad irony, however, the daughter waxes wistfully lyrical. She sees the words on the page as strangely sexualized:

> Between the dark
> legs of the capitals, moonlight, soft
> tines of the printed letter gentled

apart, nectar drawn from serif, the
self of the grown boy pouring
out.

Once again the sexual connotations in the language are too overt not to notice, except at this point the sexuality, which is always predicated upon the daughter's perception and mood, is unusually blameless, and apparently gentle. The daughter sees the sap of the young man as a surprisingly tender, fecund oozing. He is "the fresh / man kneeling in pine-needle weave" like a celebrant on a woven rug, communing with a surprisingly romantic world that is half nature, half artifice, "worshiping her." This was the father that the daughter so seldom mentions: "It was my father / good, it was my father grateful," she says, and then to underscore the fresh youth who preceded the extinct man, the daughter ends the poem with the recognition that "he wanted me to know him, he wanted / someone to know him."

"By Fire" (*BTS 75*) is another late-conceived manifesto or ars poetica. The poem represents a catharsis in the dramatic struggle with father figures, and it is an unusual meditation for Olds in the memento mori (reminder of death) tradition. A complex statement in terms of imagery and discourse, its final message is straightforward: the daughter will fight, literally to death, not to become the man who so haunts her psyche. It is a largely expressionistic message predicated upon two conceits, structural decay and the familiar private symbol of fire. The daughter is the tenor comparing herself to "an abandoned, half-wrecked building, / on a waste-lot, in winter." Unlike the vehicle of the dilapidated city scene, however, the daughter says, "I am not going / to rot." *Rot* in this context refers to the physical and spiritual degradation she witnessed in her own family. Death is inevitable, yet she will not deteriorate and collapse like an abandoned building—an image that also serves as the vehicle for the father and the grandfather, both abandoned and fallen. She then rejects the gruesome outgrowths of death in a bizarre yet creative catalog ("cauliflower, "eggshell mushroom," "fungus," "Calvinist lips blooming little / broccolis," "nails growing into curls of horn"—as if her body is composed of sprouting building materials), preferring the stillness of death to the comparative movement of fungal growth in the grave. Following this declaration the monologue moves from the exterior, future world to the familiar interior world of the daughter's psyche and her perennial struggles with the past. "But I was near," she says, "when ferment / moved, in its swerving tunnels, through my father." And this behavior (of "ferment," referring to both biological change and upheaval) she also rejects. Instead, she says, "I am going to burn I am going to pour my / body out as fire." And by the end of the poem, imagining the act of cremation in "the fire closet," the daughter compares herself to a pugilist, fighting even as she vanishes in flame. Certain poems in *The Father* ("The Mortal One," "The Urn," "His Ashes," and "The Cigars") reveal that, in fact, the father was cremated. As always the father with his failures of body, spirit, and intellect is implicitly compared to the daughter (who is always Sharon Olds on the periphery) and her tremendous success of health, motherhood, expressivity, and erudition. Forever the daughter will represent ascendant femininity and gendered morality juxtaposed against base, biologically defective masculinity. So on the one hand, "By Fire" simply contemplates death and concludes that expulsion by fire is the better way to leave the planet than the natural but horrific processes of decay; on the other hand, the poem reflects the ongoing battle of the living psyche, which, as the title indicates, is continually aflame with Oedipal conflict.

CHAPTER 4

The Mother Poems

The mother character emerges almost reluctantly from the poetry, taking shape across the canon until, like the father, she finally comes into focus in her final days. Like the father she is first referred to in the titular poem of *Satan Says* in the line "*My mother is a pimp.*" And as with the father, portraits of the mother are less than flattering. In "Tricks" (*SS* 14), the second mother poem, she is Satanic, capable of performing both simple parlor magic and witchcraft: the "eggs" that "appear in her hand" symbolize the cyclical powers of reproduction that empowers womanhood; under the same spell, however, the daughter's ovaries are blighted "black as figs." The mother is both progenitor and destroyer, granting the power to create generations and then rescinding it. Her uncanny body manifests this spiritual malevolence. When she "takes out her eyes" in "Tricks," the sockets "fill with" the essence of her being, "oil . . . bourbon and feces." And for a grand finale to this demonic magic show,

> she draws my father
> out of her cunt and puts him
> in a tall silk hat
> and he disappears.

In using such extreme imagery, Olds both expresses her typical hyperbolic rage and reifies the seemingly supernatural power of the parent, a presence that controls even reproduction and thus the health of generations. Such an obviously tainted fairy tale is further enactment of the imperative to exit (speak) "through Satan's mouth" first given voice in "Satan Says."

This power, and whatever powers of womanhood exist, are repeatedly tainted by the mother from childhood on. For instance in "The Try-Outs" (*BTS* 67)—a story of the mother's musical audition at a "downtown theater"—the mother vacuums the living room while mangling the lyrics of a mysterious aria ("*Rat!* Torturing my *BRAIN!*"); both activities are symbolic of her persona as damaged housewife. The daughter, recalling how she listened backstage to her mother's audition, cannot help but remember "the way my skin tightened, and rose, and I / cried, when she sang." Like the father's, the mother's role is to poison the domestic sphere, inflict pain on her child (unintentionally and intentionally), and then take this abuse into the public sphere. Even her voice, when raised in song, is a source of psychic damage. Other examples follow throughout the poetry. As is generally the case, the influence of the family patriarch looms behind everything women do in Olds's universe, and the daughter remembers kissing her mother's "sacred" mouth "that drew back from kissing my father." The implication is that, like the father, the mother transfers her contaminated lineage of patriarchal abuse to the daughter. In "Burn Center" (*TDATL* 37), when the mother boasts about her hospital donation, the daughter's own "hair lifts and wavers like smoke." The daughter compares herself to a burn victim, "without skin, walking around scalded / raw." Yet, drawing an ironic allegory between herself and children in the burn center who receive the benefit of the mother's largesse, the daughter complains that "no one gave me / a strip of gauze or a pat of butter to / melt on my crackling side."

Olds is seldom specific about forces that shape her characters; details are sparse about the people themselves. Their physical beings, their history, and their character traits are generally rendered through metaphor and paraphrase. Readers are given scenarios, snippets of dialogue, paraphrase, and narrations limited by the brevity of lyric poetry. From these limited essentials, they are nevertheless invited to reconstruct specific characters. What Olds accomplishes by this reduction of character, without the stage directions of extended literary forms, is the essence of art since modernism: readers are given the chance to invest their own imaginations into patterns constructed by the artist. Still the mother is almost unfathomable. Virtually nothing is known about her. In "Mother" (*TUR* 101) the daughter performs a rare discursion on her person:

> Whatever she was to me, she was
> the human caught in something she could hardly
> bear, she was like a flying keening
> being, limed and jessed, a small
> soprano of the trees.

The metaphors are evocative but cliché ("caught in something") or abstract to the point of vagueness ("soprano of the trees"), and this tropology of indistinctness relegates her to a figurative distance unusual for such a well-worn character.

It would be easy to dismiss the mother as an example of agitprop or as a foil. Yet as with her other characters, Olds is masterful in expanding intimate experience into commentary about culture and politics. For example, in "The Learner" (*TUR* 97), the mother finds "her late husband's / flag in the attic." This token of her past triggers recollections of many of the finer points of human interaction—patriotism and the care the late husband received following a stroke—at the same time that the flag is a symbol of repressed womanhood: the mother "sounds like a soldier who has known / no other life." This blending of the political, the personal, and the symbolic alludes to the gestalt of personhood within the American milieu. Again the hegemony of the patriarchy lurks in the background. Fathers are associated with dominance and violence—forces that, like the flag symbol, are obliquely linked to human ideologies, masculinity foremost. In "Mother" the daughter identifies her as "a kind of sister, in thrall / to three fathers—mine, and hers, / and Our Heavenly." *Sister* is a coded word in feminist discourse, and despite the antagonism the daughter feels toward her mother, the daughter also feels a kindred victimization. She realizes that "if I sing, I sing from her," a possible allusion to "The Try-Outs." This complicated matrix of energies is what shapes womanhood in the poetry, and Olds's brilliance as a commentator is apparent even as, once again, the tropology is arguably bathetic. Moreover her characters often display just this level of duality, both as phantoms of fleshed-out people and as allegorical figures that stand for larger political causes. Her ability to draw characters that reify complex states of being, essentially illustrating how the macrocosm affects the individual, is part of how she exceeds the limitations associated with the confessional mode.

At the root of these dramas and pathologies is the panoptic culture of the postwar United States and its unintended degradation of women. In "The Meal" (*TGC* 27) the mother is apostrophized "sitting with your excellent skeletal posture / facing that plate with the one scoop of cottage cheese on it, / forcing yourself to eat, though you did not want to live." She is a dark satire of the devoted housewife, obsessed with outward appearance, constrained, hypocritical, and disillusioned. And the daughter responds (as did much of the Baby Boomer generation) with sexual liberation. "What I remember," the daughter says, "is your / spoon moving like the cock moving in the / body of the girl waking to the power of her pleasure." The mother often assumes the role, presumably unwittingly, of provocateur, again evoking the line from "Satan Says," "*my mother is a pimp.*"

However, in the mother poems, these allusions to sex and reproduction can also suggest the unionizing power of womanhood. In "The Moment" (*TDATL* 42), a memory poem about her first menstruation, the daughter descends into the basement, "past the grandfather clock" and "below the / level of the earth"—symbols of patriarchy and the geography of oppression—where she finds the mother in a deliberately clichéd depiction of the harried housewife, her hands "thrust deep in soapy water." When the daughter explains that she has gotten her period, the small, worn woman that is the mother reaches for her daughter joyfully, her hands covered by "tiny delicate bubbles like seeds." Biology, the power of reproduction, turns symbols of marginalization (bubbles) into symbols of growth (seeds) and provides a generational link between the two, one of the few times this is portrayed in the early poetry. Menstruation—"the dark Egyptian stain"—marks the end of childhood and the onset of womanhood, an event that creates the possibility of connection. Both are now fertile woman and can bestow the ultimate gift of life. The power to give birth is emphatically celebrated in Olds's poetry and always harbors romantic possibilities of rebirth and renewal. However, what is disturbing in the scenario (because pain and psychological dysfunction are seldom far away in Olds's universe) is that the mother has been demoted in a sense to the lowest levels of the household and to rather traditional matronly duties, doing the laundry by hand. Such an elevation (the gift of fertility), when paired with a descent into a symbolic underworld (the basement), signifies the complexity of their relationship and the complexity of women's world. The geography of the poem also speaks to the different expectations between the generations during late midcentury when this narrative putatively takes place (Olds herself would have been a teenager during the presidency of Dwight Eisenhower). Once again the mother is thematically linked to the father: both characters are relegated to the grotesque and hampered by the physical environment of the household.

Implicitly and explicitly the detrimental effects of culture are standard themes in Olds's poetry, and yet she is unstinting in the denunciation of her characters on a personal level. Confessional poetry is predicated on family dysfunction and its lasting effects. Nowhere is this more apparent than in "The Elder Sister" (*TDATL* 48), a constructed memory of one of Olds's rarest characters. Through the daughter's highly subjective focalizing lens, childbirth is transformed into peculiar violence: the mother's muscles squeeze the sister's brain as she travels down the birth canal. Such brain damage, the poem implies, accounts for the sister's warped personality. Here the birth process, generally greeted with reverence, is a brutal act, a harbinger of the psychic violence of the family. It is also a very funny, if adolescent, analysis.

Surprisingly given her sour, pathetic, incompetent, antifeminist, and satanic beginnings, the portrayals of the mother have evolved sympathetically across the poetry, an evolution the character of the father does not share. A prime example is "Visiting My Mother's College" (*TW* 3), in which the daughter pilgrimages to the geographical location memorialized in "I Go Back to May 1937." Here she imagines the mother as a fresh young coed "on her stomach, still a child, studying / diligently for finals" and rinsing her hair with lemon before the dance "so the interior of her / tiny room was flecked with sour bright citrus." Again, like the fresh-faced boy that was once the father, the mother, Olds implies, was once a genuine young person yet to be victimized by her life as an adult, a situation ostensibly created by the father. Likewise, symbolized by the "sour bright" presence in her dorm room before the social rite of the dance, the mother's natural self is both energetic and bitter, attributes that poison her personality later on. The companion poem to "Visiting My Mother's College," "My Parents' Wedding Night, 1937" (*TW* 4), is also a constructed memory of the mother's loss of her "maidenhead." "The war / had not yet begun," the daughter says, and her parents "lay and slept / in blood and peace, no one knew what was coming." "The war" refers to World War II, which altered geopolitics forever, but also to the private war between these two individuals that will dominate the micropolitics of the family. Once again the microcosm of human relations is a synecdoche for greater political violence, centering the family as the prime mover of culture and history.

The mother's guilt, confession, and clemency all occur in one poem, "After 37 Years My Mother Apologizes for My Childhood" (*TGC* 43). As the title suggests, in this vignette the mother performs a mea culpa with the typical bathos of Olds's family narratives. The scene and drama are fairly simple: the mother runs weeping toward the daughter as if to embrace her. As the mother "tilted toward" her as if "trying to walk through fire" (again utilizing Olds's principal trope for masculine psychic violence), the daughter experiences a cinematic catharsis: "The sky seemed to be splintering like a window / someone is bursting into or out of." Clearly the psychological tableau has changed, but the daughter cannot tell whether a new conception has entered or a barrier has been exited—the symbolism of the broken window contains both of these possibilities. For the second time in the poetry, the mother's eyes fill "with terrible liquid," but not the "bourbon and feces" of before; at this moment, seven years after Olds portrayed the mother as a demon in her first book, the old woman's eyes brighten with "balls of mercury from a broken thermometer." Here, almost cartoonish in its evocation, the mother has symbolically boiled over and burst, and the daughter has little recourse but to grant pardon. There is, as is generally the case, a virtually Manichaean dichotomy in which the daughter is the arbiter of moral outrage and the parents are justly condemned. Yet this experience creates a new motif that finds fruition in *One Secret Thing.* Unmoored by the emotional catharsis and undone by pity, the daughter loses the force of her own manifesto against family dysfunction. "I could not see what I would do with the rest of my life," the daughter apostrophizes the mother; "I hardly knew what I / said or who I would be now that I had forgiven you."

The mother transforms into a flesh-and-blood woman—one who is still judged and found to be flawed but is a sympathetic character nevertheless—primarily in two books, *The Wellspring* (1996) and *One Secret Thing* (2008). The mother is represented as a growing presence in *One Secret Thing,* primarily in two sections of the book: "The Cannery," a chapter that deals with bittersweet childhood memories, and "Cassiopeia," a sequence of poems centering around the mother as she nears death. In "The Cannery" the mother comes into and out of the poetic frame in a series of memory, tableau, and portrait poems, all typical of Olds's style, as well as surreal poems of the sort Olds uses more rarely to portray intense emotional states. The section is concerned with the role of women in the world, and the mother is often an unwitting foil for strong feminist women.

The first poem of the section, "The Cannery, 1942–1945" (23), casts the mother in a rare moment of feminist solidarity. As the dates in the title suggest, World War II, and the resultant entry of women into the workforce, hangs significantly in the background. The daughter recalls a cannery run by a woman whose bodily strength and short statue personify her relative position within society. Nevertheless "she moved with a purpose, / there in her war-effort kitchen." The daughter mistakes the sterilizers and pistons as the woman's own inventions and admires her intimacy with the operation; the machines seemed like "the workings of her mind," as if purpose and environment are synchronistic in the human story. This scenario ends in tragedy, however: "When the war ended, / and the little factory was dismantled, she killed / herself." As is often the case, Olds's meaning is overt and arguably melodramatic. Still her point about gender politics is made. Here, for one of the few times in the poetry, the daughter is given a gift of strength, albeit from one who is the mother's antithesis. When her mother holds the daugher up to the "woman Hephaistos" who runs the cannery, the experience is one of being blessed by a female idol who, with her mechanical ability, personal industry, and passion, is a counterpart to the stunted character of the mother. Perhaps inadvertently, certainly ironically, the mother has shown the daughter a feminine role model. This sense of ambivalent gratitude does not last long, however.

In "Diagnosis" (*OST* 24) the daughter describes how her mother took her to the pediatrician as an infant because she thought the child "was Possessed" (referencing Olds's poem "Possessed"); instead the doctor pronounces the daughter's worrisome condition to be a sense of humor. The daughter's sarcasm is illustrated by her paraphrase: "Ohhh, she said, and took me / back to the house where that sense would be tested / and found to be incurable." The extended exclamation dramatizes the mother's incomprehension and humorlessness. The companion poem "At Night" (25) expands the portrait of the mother as a clumsy, repressed autocrat. The scenario is the generally comforting childhood ritual of being tucked in at bedtime. In the adversarial relationship between the daughter and the mother, however, it turns into a kind of oddly sexualized (though not overtly sexual) abuse. The sheets, the daughter remembers, "pressed me like a fierce / restraint," making her into her mother's "squeeze." The mother, "made of desire leashed," turns this codependency to a restrained violence. In this perversion of childhood ritual, the daughter's psyche expresses itself with some perversity, and she says of her sister and herself, "we were like parts of a / sexual part, squeaky and sweet." The daughter's psychology is again tied to the sublimated rage of a disassociated and yet codependent parent; disabled in some not entirely defined manner, the emotionally hobbled child seeks healing through compulsive sexual release.

Later in the same section, in "Freezer" (*OST* 36) the daughter forms a vague analogy between the mother and a "murder-cannibal." She charges that her mother, like a storybook witch, fattened her "until it was time / to cook me," though she did so unknowingly, as she was "robbed of a moral sense that way." Unaccountably her presence in the daughter's life is allegorized by a magazine about a killer secreted away in a drawer. It is as if this penchant for barbarism is a text that the daughter hides in her own private recesses. She grimly links reproduction and the act of a mother preparing to eat her children, a motif of classical mythology that accentuates the mythological themes of the collection. The textual presence of such horror allows the daughter to focus her own feelings of violence and victimization, to envision and come to terms with the psychic cannibals in her own life. "It comforts me that the story is available," she says, "at any moment, accounted for, not / dangerously unthought of." By relating to the murder-cannibal, the daughter somehow brings her own emotions out into the open, although it is not clear that this provides any solace. Once again Olds has amplified the emotional relevance of the situation into hyperbole, comparing a problematic childhood to the gruesome activities of a serial killer. The mother in this equation metaphorically keeps body parts, presumably chopped from members of her own family, in a freezer for later consumption. And once again the Saturn myth, with its motif of infanticide, becomes relevant. The poem ends with one of the more startling metaphors in Olds's oeuvre, when the daughter describes an early memory of sitting in a bathtub with her mother and seeing her vagina as "a mouth, a youthfully bearded mouth / with blood on it."

This relationship is a psychological battleground that spills over into actual physical conflict in "The Couldn't" (39), a narrative in which the daughter will not submit to corporal punishment because she does not want to remove her sanitary belt. The *couldn't* of the poem is actually much more appropriately a *wouldn't*. Through this conflict of privacy and dignity, not coincidentally associated with the onset of menstruation, the daughter first realizes her ability to fight back. Accidentally, perhaps, Olds has appropriated a seminal tenet of feminist discourse that conceives of reproduction as a source of female empowerment. However women's bodies in "The Couldn't" are complicated symbols of both violence and freedom. As with "The Moment," menstruation is the cycle that joins mother and daughter ("our bodies called to each other"), and yet the menstrual flow that signals the onset of womanhood is couched in metaphors of bloodshed: the women "brought each other bleeding off in the / waste of the power of creation." The natural process of shedding the endometrial lining becomes a battle metaphor, a reminder of life squandered.

From this point in *One Secret Thing*, the vignettes of the mother begin to evolve, sometimes painfully, sometimes surprisingly, into a portrait of a fully fleshed dramatic persona. In "Royal Beauty Bright" (55), the storyline of the mother has its second major development, the onset of her illness. As with the poems in *The Father*, light is a motif of the waning life force, and as in the poems of the father's illness, pathos is created by healing ministrations. "Royal Beauty Bright" atomizes the accoutrements—the "oxygen, catheter, blood-pressure cuff, / heart monitor," "wires," and "tubes"—that fashion modern medicine. This life-saving apparatus actually turns into painful restraints, and the daughter describes the needles of the IV tearing the mother's arms as she attempts to hoist her "ninety pounds" over her bed frame. Suddenly the mother inspires empathy. Five-point restraints tie her down as she becomes unreasonable in her delirium (though no more so than at other points in her life). "Royal Beauty Bright" offers an overarching conceit for the mother's entire existence as her irrationality, her combativeness, her self-destructiveness, and her constraining life forces are manifestly symbolized by the ironic inhumanity of modern medicine.

"Royal Beauty Bright" also includes the daughter's first acts of compassion toward her mother. In earlier poems, those predicated upon childhood memories, the daughter is often the unwilling consolation for the mother's excessive woe, as in "What If God" (*TGC* 25), or the recipient of her sublimated aggression, as in "At Night" and "Freezer." Yet in this scenario she is dutiful and comforting; she stays by the mother's bedside, singing "the old carols" until "the morphine took her." Her "five-pointed flesh" suggests the kind of star that children are taught to draw, and the poem ends with lyrics from "We Three Kings," the same carol the poem's title is taken from. The title plays with the symbolic relevance of light in Olds's poetry and the notion of the mother as a household queen or religious figure. As with the father's illness, at the moment of her mortality, the mother becomes a figure of aristocratic or deific tropology.

In the next poem of the narrative sequence, "The Riser" (57), readers learn that the mother has almost died of toxic shock—a condition in which the body reacts to bacterial toxins in the bloodstream. She recovers in the course of the narrative and is compared, somewhat surprisingly, to Jesus Christ. Interestingly the daughter narrates this vignette in the present tense. She invokes images of light, religious similes, and recollections of childhood in a plainspoken, syntactically simple sentence joined to brief adjectival and participial phrases that belie the complexity of the tropology. Olds's understated intricacy is reinforced by her tone, which is conversational, even homespun. She describes the rising of her mother simply:

> Now she stands by the bed,
> gaunt, slightly luminous, the
> hospital gown hanging in blue
> folds, like the picture of Jesus-come-back
> in my choir book.

Olds is not a religious poet, but as an American poet she understands the matrix of feelings associated with the Christ figure, and as a personal poet she understands the intense emotions of a parent on the brink of death. This is yet another manifestation in the poetry of the daughter's longing for parental communion. Siblings are virtually absent in the plotline except as antagonistic foils (the sister) or extensions of the family dysfunction (the brother), but the parents are repeatedly granted godhood, or a near amalgam, when recollected in mourning. So long as the daughter is separated from her household deities, she enacts a doctrine of frustrated longing.

The daughter's feelings from this point on vacillate among dread, relief, and ironic tension in "Pansy Coda" (60) and "The Dead" (64), the next poems two in the sequence. "Pansy Coda" revolves around the triggering image of flowers that the mother tended. Seeing the blossoms, the daughter experiences a rare moment of soothing self-reflection:

> I am tired of hating myself, tired
> of loathing. I want to be carried in a petal
> sling, sling of satin and cream,
> I want to be dazed, I want the waking sleep.

In "The Dead," however, she admits her own sense of liberation at the prospect of her mother's death:

For a moment I see
it would not be an entirely bad thing
if my mother died. How interesting
to be in the world when she was not.

Once again the mother poems have thematic counterparts in the father poems. In both series the narrator finds affection in the wake of death primarily because she is free of the parents' bullying. Thus death brings the freedom to love. In both mother and father poems, the presence of mortality jars the daughter's sublimated affection and forces her, almost guiltily, to admit her own and her parents' human qualities. Again the concept of a personal poet is relevant in this instance—the admission, while it could be considered unsavory or even disturbing, marks an honest revelation of a unique emotional response.

"Good Measure" (67), the culminating poem of "The Cannery," is much like "deep image" poetry in that the narrative seeks correspondences between the physical and spiritual worlds through significant, loosely associated images. Sleeping in the mother's house, the daughter awakens, somewhat mysteriously, into a liminal state between consciousness and dream. Like the pansies in daylight, luminous nighttime images of the household trigger a series of free associations. Light, once again, symbolizes life, but the images are abstract, almost as if the daughter herself is unsure of their meaning. The "luminous wedge" on the back of her hand is "a patch of Alamogordo— / the new-risen moon, the last quarter." It is an interesting pairing of images. The first image alludes to the site in New Mexico where the Trinity nuclear tests fused acres of trinitite, the green glass created by the heat of atomic detonation, often referred to as "Alamogordo glass," evoking the aftermath of fire, the self-destructive and warlike aspects of human nature. As with any aftermath of nuclear explosion, the landscape is irradiated and dangerous. To this she yokes the second image, the new moon. There is always the danger of being cliché, particularly in poetry that deals with love or that metaphorizes the moon in any form. Olds manages to avoid these literary pitfalls and actually expands the symbol of the moon into a new connotation. In a poem that deals with the mother's self-imposed psychology ("she could dwell / on herself in bitterness, or dwell on / herself in hope") and the daughter's evolving yet unresolved reconciliation of the childhood she laments across nine volumes ("lately, there's a / motion, diurnal—when drenched with attention / she might turn to me, with affection"), the moon symbolizes love that hovers between anger (the darkness) and the luminosity of life and forgiveness (the light).

They call the half moon the last
quarter, staying faithful to the back bulge,

> to the edge between too little and too much,
> the narrow calcium line neither roasting
> nor freezing.

Here the moon symbolizes her conflicted feelings. Love is in its "last quarter," the end of life and of affection, and the daughter expresses dedication to the dark side of the moon, "the back bulge" of rage repeatedly explored through the seasons of her poetry. At the same time, the image harks back to the larval moon hanging over the mother as the stepfather was carted away in an ambulance, leaving the mother in her new life.

Such hopeful correspondences provide no closure, however, and Olds returns to the themes of the unhappy childhood overshadowed by father figures. She uses the biblical legend of Adam's "sore resentful rib" as an allusion to the ever-present threat of the patriarchy. Like the Genesis 2:21 account of Eve's creation—emblematic of women's secondary nature in the long history of patriarchal mythology—the overarching bone house of masculinity intrudes into the feminine subconscious. Except for its inhospitableness for human life, the daughter muses, "one could make one's home / on that border" of the moon's liminal stage. The daughter is unmoored by experience, floating in space, and "Good Measure" becomes another ars poetica in which she describes herself as a "nomad offspring of the stone opal . . . singing, across the night." Olds ends on the metapoetic statement, "Here is my pleynt," signifying the intractability of time through the archaic spelling of the word.

The final two sections of *One Secret Thing,* "Cassiopeia" and the titular "One Secret Thing," follow the mother's story as she dies from a brain tumor and is cremated, her ashes scattered at sea. The mother speaks for the first time, sometimes in paraphrase, sometimes in direct quotation, as certain other aspects of her life—that she was married a second time and was a high school music teacher—are revealed. While the ostensible subjects of the eight numbered poems in "Cassiopeia" are the mother and her struggle with age and mortality, as with much of Olds's poetry, the real subject is the daughter and her battle for self-esteem. This self-referential and self-objectifying aspect of Olds's art is her clearest link to the confessional aesthetic.

Unlike many of the best-educated poets, Olds is not a writer who uses her literary expertise as an Emerson scholar with an Ivy League doctorate to provide material for erudite allusions. "Cassiopeia," however, obviously draws inspiration from classical mythology. While there are several versions of the story, the essentials of the myth all revolve around a vain Ethiopian queen who insults the sea nymphs by suggesting that she is as beautiful as they are. Enraged and indignant, they complain to the sea god, Poseidon, who sends the monster

Cetus to destroy Cassiopeia's country. In order to save his kingdom, King Cepheus, Cassiopeia's husband, chains their daughter, Andromeda, to a rock as a sacrifice. On the flying horse Pegasus, the hero Perseus (son of a princess, Danaë, who was imprisoned in a golden tower by her father and impregnated by Zeus) rescues Andromeda by killing the monster. Olds does not directly reference the myth; instead she leaves the reader to infer the analogy: the mother is Cassiopeia, the father is Cepheus, the sea monster symbolizes culture, and the daughter, apparently, is Andromeda. Significantly the cover of the 2008 Borzoi Books edition shows the gold outline of a queen seated on a throne, scepter in hand, against a background of stars in the distinctive W shape of the constellation Cassiopeia. In the myth Poseidon, presumably enraged at the loss of his sea monster, punishes Cassiopeia by tying her to a chair in the stars, forming the eponymous constellation. Ironically the queen's vanity will always be assuaged by her position in the cosmos, a metatextual implication about the mother character. Cassiopeia's punishment also aligns with the daughter's own memory of being tied to a chair as a child. Metatextually and symbolically, the role of the punisher has come full circle, and now the daughter has tied the mother to a chair where her vanity can be discussed, admired (by admirers of the poet's art), and yet denigrated.

The "Cassiopeia" section begins its narrative sequence with a depiction of death: "He Is Taken Away" (71) is a tableau poem of the final moments of the mother's second husband. As with many of Olds's memory poems, a simple scenario is rendered in plainspoken yet symbolically resonant language. At midnight, beneath a larval moon (which signifies the underdeveloped state of the mother's psyche), the stepfather is taken away in an ambulance. The stepfather is one of the most mysterious characters in Olds's cast; he has exactly one poem dedicated to him earlier in *One Secret Thing,* and it is not a flattering portrait. "Paterfamilias" (42) describes a lecherous, elderly, drunken, and predatory stepfather who shouts, "Your mother has the best damn fanny / in the house," and then orders the daughter and the sister to turn around so they too can be judged. He is a bear-hugging, buttocks slapping, stereotypical chauvinist whose eyes shine "like eyes of devils and fascists in horror / comic books." Somehow this masculine monstrosity mirrors and fulfills the mother's need for gratuitous affirmation, "as if they belonged / on earth—maybe owned it, and every creature on it." A paterfamilias is the head of a household, the eldest male, who traditionally had unquestioned rule of the family. The title indicates the relative autocracy of this man, the kind of man that represents the worst of the 1950s male. His death is foretold in "The Learner," a poem in *The Unswept Room,* and his absence is noted in "Pansy Coda."

In "He Is Taken Away," he is disposed of quickly, with barely an expositional nod, as the ambulance departs. Uninterested in any judgment of the character's worth, Olds gives the stepfather a final, deserved snub and turns her attention to the character that emerges as her fullest portrait to date. The mother now fills the focalizing frame. She is found standing still in the street, metaphorically linked to the darkness and "the moon / like a larva." Sexualizing the gestalt as is her wont, the daughter says that her mother "looked so alive, so vivid, / like a woman motionless at the moment of orgasm." This is an ironic juxtaposition of life and death, mortality and sexuality. All these are present at the moment the mother is freed of masculine influence; sexual climax is a metaphor for freedom as well as the revival of generative power. Sexuality is a source of rebellion and rejuvenation in Olds's poetry, particularly when associated with freedom from the mother's psychological grip, and now the one-time oppressor gets her own new life. In this regard the two main antagonists in Olds's canon share similarities in their ability to generate sexual tension. Like the father during his death struggles, emotional strain manifests itself as light bleeding through the dying mother's body; in "He is Taken Away," this manifestation, "glowing, slightly, / from the inner ambulance light," is only on the surface, as if the reality of the mother is only skin-deep. At the same time, the mother is rarified and objectified as "a scrimshaw Crusader / chess-piece rotated slowly on its base." She can only move in prescribed patterns, and in the depths of her shock, she appears to be constructed of hard, inorganic materials, "wax or ivory or marble." The daughter perceives that some profound as yet undefined change has occurred and senses a new epic potential in the mother "like / Homer ready to be led around the known globe." This transformation from inert matter and mechanical motion to epic adventurer signifies the beginning of a recognition on the daughter's part: she now perceives that her mother—the dreadful character who tied her to a chair, drunkenly battled the father, and lay weeping on top of her—sees the world anew somehow. Surprisingly, finally, the mother has found a voice.

In "The Music" (72), the next poem in the sequence, the mother actually speaks, albeit in words related by the daughter: "*I'm not unhappy, / she says, this is better for me than church.*" Again she seems to be gaining a measure of organic life; her voice is "the low singing / of a watered plant long not watered." As is typical of Olds's poetic discourse, however, the effect of revelation creates introspection bordering on self-indulgence. "I had wanted never to stop blaming her," the daughter admits, "like eating hard-shelled animals / at mid-molt," seeming to link her mother to a hermit crab without its shell. And again, as is typical of Olds's poetry, the discourse becomes metapoetic: "I think /

I had thought I would falter if I forgave my mother." As the later poems will show, this is a prescient statement; the daughter's antagonism toward her parents had been an animating principle from the first, and now this antipathy is in jeopardy; she is actually becoming sympathetic toward her own antagonists, and this implies danger toward her sense of self, predicated, as it has been, on antipathy toward her mother. By the end of "The Music," the daughter achieves a qualified empathy, even admiration, saluting the mother as "scout of the mortal, heart / breaking into solo." She is out on her own now, the daughter seems to say, fighting spiritual constraint, even though the trail still must be forged.

In the next two poems, "The Ecstatic" (74) and "Two Late Dialogues" (75), Olds's dark wit humanizes the mother. Unlike the cruel, codependent parent of earlier poems, she is portrayed in "The Ecstatic" with an affectionate observation tinged with sadness: "On her first antidepressant, my mother / is adorable." When she actually speaks, she is slightly irreverent, almost whimsical: "I've got it on, I'm all dingus'd up, / I knew you would want to know that I'm all / hooked up!" This frail portrait is juxtaposed to the "Leviathan" that the daughter wants "to draw out . . . with a hook," a metaphor for need and a rare biblical allusion in Olds's work. This is followed by quotations from Job 38:4 and 38:7 in which God reminds Job of his relative insignificance next to God's celestial might. "I was there," the daughter says, standing next to Job "with my mother." Suddenly the "ecstatic" of the poem is the daughter herself, worshiping at the altar of the deific mother she previously disparaged and lampooned. She may also allude to the ending of the story of Job, in which Job's family, health, and wealth are restored to him as a reward for his faith.

In the companion poem to "The Ecstatic," "Two Late Dialogues," subtitled "Mom as Comet," the comet Hale-Bopp embodies the mother's fear of an existential universe—although it seems certain that she would not have used this term. Rather her incomprehension forms the poem's central conceit. She perceives Hale-Bopp as an omen of her own impending mortality, "*a force, / a nameless force*" aimed directly at her. Her personification of a natural phenomenon suggests the limitations of her intellect, even as a sympathetic character, and it gives insight into her worldview as the celebrated comet (one of the brightest ever recorded) becomes a harbinger of worldly destruction. Forced to contemplate the universe, possibly for the first time, the mother sees only annihilation. Yet again, paradoxically, this overwrought emotion gives her her own force in the world.

> She looked like a comic actor
> doing a drunk, she looked like a tough

kid on a corner, amusing the others,
a person with an identity.

Identity has so often been at the center of Olds's reflections—as illustrated through the characters' lives, as a cultural or gender construct, even the identity of the arts themselves—and at this moment the mother finally achieves a measure of personhood, albeit juvenile and clownish. The inclusion of Hale-Bopp dates the conversation described in this poem to 1996–97, when the comet was at perihelion. As is often the case with Olds's poetic renderings ostensibly of her own experiences, the retelling follows the actual event by a decade or more.

Olds allows her characters to assert their complex, contradictory personalities through miniature productions of their own words and actions. "Her Creed" (77), the fifth poem in the "Cassiopeia" sequence and the second of two short dialogue poems, portrays the mother essentially as an ironic, unaware philosopher who represents the poles of female experience; her lack of self-realization mirrors the paradoxes of her own life, her relationship to the daughter, and her parallel roles as creator and moral guardian. "*I believe / in the creation of / the criminal, / the evil people,*" the mother says; however, she follows this with the affirmation that "*everyone born is a miracle,*" suggesting, on the one hand, that the worst aspects of human nature are inborn and, on the other, that life is precious nevertheless under any circumstances. The dialogue that follows is a largely empty exchange of platitudes and non sequiturs, emblematic of the superficiality of the characters' communication, yet it belies the more serious familial and feminist interactions that fuel much of Olds's poetry. The moment is contextualized by the hegemony of science over life and the masculine imperative that employs it.

Over and over,
these days, she tells me they never will be able
to assemble real flesh, in a dish, not flesh
with spirit—the men cannot make happen
what happened in her body.

Once again science is a dehumanizing force, particularly as it relates to reproduction. The mother, meanwhile, has suddenly appropriated the power of regeneration so closely associated with the biological power of women, that which stands against the patriarchy in Olds's poetry. This is a surprisingly spiritual moment for the mother. Here she is associated with the affirmation of life, and the daughter responds with surprising affection.

In the following poems, however, the daughter resumes her textual battle. The next poem in the sequence, "Warily, Sportsman!" (78), takes its title from

Walt Whitman's 1860 poem "The Sleepers," which also provides the poem's epigraph: "Warily, sportsman! though I lie so sleepy and sluggish, my tap is death." Whitman's poem is famous for its imaginative nightscape overlooking human industry, good and bad, and the allusion here is an interesting counterpart to the Whitmanesque sense of community: the lines Olds quotes warn of impending mortality and implied violence toward the speaker. In "Warily, Sportsman!" the mother betrays her own penchant for meting out abuse that leads, symbolically, to death (she worries that a kick to the stepfather's shin caused his stroke)—a bit of hyperbolic humor on spiritual violence and the destruction of the individual. As if fulfilling the warning of Whitman's language from 150 years earlier, the daughter says of the mother that "no one hit her back / until today—by-blow of this page, / coldcock to her little forehead." Likewise, in "Little End Ode" (80), the sixth poem in the "Cassiopeia," sequence the daughter reignites her private battle of words with the mother: "As soon as I / dared, around fifty, I called her, to myself, / the A-word."

This passive-aggressive tug-of-war culminates in "*Something Is Happening*" (81), the penultimate poem of the sequence, in which the mother's brain tumor is announced. A portrait of the mother's psychological isolation ("She's so sheerly lonely / she is like the one member of a tribe") and the daughter's unremitting judgment ("It was painful to know her / such a feral one, untrained, unmothered"), this meditation nevertheless suggests a degree of sympathy. The title foreshadows the mystery of mortality; both mother and daughter can sense the coming of "something . . . bigger than love, bigger than aloneness." In this state, as the mother teeters toward her end, the daughter's imagery is strangely geographic, dealing with fields, deserts, "unscanned rivers of asteroids," and even planets on which the mother's failing body would be beautiful. Such private symbology is ripe for explication—except that "*Something Is Happening*" provides few specific correlatives to the symbols, almost as if the daughter cannot parse the complicated landscape generated by her emotions. At best she can only return to her hyperbolic reading of the scenario, and the mother is "not just death, but the truth, / her self, soon to be completed." The fact that Olds separates the reflexive pronoun *herself* into an attributive pronoun and noun, from a closed form to an open form, syntactically illustrates the sundered nature of the mother and indicates who (or what) has been found: the mother finds her true *self* through the act of dying; the being at the center of her consciousness is "completed" in death. Throughout Old's poetry the mother has been portrayed, rightly or wrongly, as an agent of discord. Yet here she is aligned with the ultimate destructive cycles in the universe, revealed in cosmic signs and omens. In the end the big thing that is coming is death itself, a force greater than any human industry, good or bad.

In the eighth and last poem of the sequence, also titled "Cassiopeia" (82), the daughter has a revelation that "she was not meant to be a mother, / she never got to be a child until now." This is as close to reconciliation as the daughter allows herself to get. The mother's character, like the father's, can be explained through her own damaged childhood, and the circle of dysfunction is connected. This insight presages a role reversal as the daughter (who once described her mother as a bourbon-and-feces-filled monstrosity) now imagines herself as the keeper of a simple, stupid, inoffensive life. She sees herself as "an old shepherd on a hill" and the mother as "my lamb, / who sickened so long, my first lamb, is gamboling." The Christian iconography appears rather heavy-handed at this point, and the insight into the mother's psyche could be considered cliché. At the same time, Olds has returned to her theme of familial lineage and the spiritual poverty of a damaged childhood. It is only now that the mother has a kindly overseer—a surrogate parent—that she is free of the psychological constraints of her past.

The fifth section of *One Secret Thing,* which shares its title with the collection, follows the path of the mother's final days. These last recollections begin with the highly symbolic scenario of "Still Life" (87), a metacritique on the life of a poet and the artifice of poetry itself. A still-life painting is a depiction of inanimate objects arranged in a pattern, generally anything that does not move or is dead. "At moments almost thinking of her," the daughter reflects, "I was moving through the still life museum." This is symbolic of the artist who memorializes life-in-death, even as literal life and death compete outside the frame: as the daughter wades through an imagined gallery of paintings, the mother suffers a stroke and begins her real-world death march. As the mother "raised her hands to her temples," then "screamed, and fell to her bedroom floor," the daughter says, "I / wandered, calm, among oysters, and walnuts . . . a golden smiling skull." This overt reference to the medieval memento mori tradition implicates the daughter for her supposed vanity; it is a provisional admission of guilt. For the first time (among a number of firsts for Olds in this collection), the mother is portrayed with complete sympathy, and the daughter accepts, volunteers actually, her own culpability—even if this latter dynamic is only implicated through the buffering medium of literature.

"Still Life" has an odd correlation to W. H. Auden's "Musée des Beaux Arts," also an ekphrastic poem about the relationship between life, death, and art. Auden's title in French means "Museum of Fine Arts," which is also the name of the museum in Brussels where Pieter Brueghel's (1525–69) painting *Landscape with the Fall of Icarus* hangs. In the myth from Ovid's *Metamorphosis,* the adolescent Icarus disobeys his father's instructions and flies too close to the sun, melting his wax wings and plunging to his death in the ocean.

For Auden the story provides a fable about the real triviality of human travail. Auden's poem begins:

> About suffering they were never wrong,
> The old Masters: how well they understood
> Its human position: how it takes place
> While someone else is eating or opening a window
>   or just walking dully along.

In Brueghel's painting Icarus falls almost unnoticed in the corner of the panel—his two white legs are glimpsed vanishing into the surf—signifying the insignificance of this mythical event in the midst of human industry. Above Icarus a plowman, who takes the majority of the frame, plows his field, and a massive galleon heads toward the horizon. Auden summarizes the action this way:

> the ploughman may
> Have heard the splash, the forsaken cry,
> But for him it was not an important failure; the sun shone
> As it had to on the white legs disappearing into the green
> Water, and the expensive delicate ship that must have seen
> Something amazing, a boy falling out of the sky,
> Had somewhere to get to and sailed calmly on.

Auden's point is that, while the mundane events of life trudge on, someone somewhere is dying, torturing or being tortured, and achieving the impossible. The rest of ordinary humanity must simply plow on through the necessary business of the day.

Olds's "Still Life" echoes this sentiment: despite the daughter's mounting loss, the world continues, a seeming paradox symbolized by art that portrays death. She refers to the long tradition of painting dead rabbits as hunting trophies (examples include William Harnett's *After the Hunt* and Jan Weenix's *Still Life with Game*) with the image of a "wild flayed / hare strung up by one foot like a dancer / leaping." The mother is both the dead hare and the dancer here, and the poem ends on a final admission of guilt: "she lay there and I walked / blind through music." As this section in *One Secret Thing* makes clear, the daughter repeatedly paints the mother as neurotic, self-interested, and ill-spoken—but for the first time she acknowledges she has turned this fellow human being into an art form lying still on the page. Now she returns flesh to the character, focalizes her lens back on a living woman replete with human faults and frailties. Later in "Satin Maroon" (96) the daughter explicates her new theme of the mother as victim of her own childhood:

I saw
she had always been alone—fatherless,
mismothered—and not without her own
valiant spirit.

The trauma of childhood is an overarching force in Olds's poetry, and her work continues its terrible critique of the family. What is different in this case is the effect of empathy: she has intertwined her themes of compassion, even for a former antagonist, with the rejuvenating power of family.

This new thematic construct has its most overt incarnation in the title poem, "One Secret Thing" (88). Given so many previous poems about the cosmos and death, it is a surprisingly quiet recollection of a seemingly insignificant event. Standing watch at the mother's deathbed, the daughter moistens her lips with a small amount of Vaseline. At this moment, when the mother is at her most vulnerable, the daughter senses her essential being, "something less unlike my mother than / anything else on earth," and finds that, in the simple act of wetting her lips, "I worked / for my motherhood, my humanhood." This poem is a corollary to Olds's best-known poem of her father's illness, "The Glass," in which the phlegm-filled water glass at the dying father's bedside becomes the focus of the daughter's intense emotional strain; in "One Secret Thing" the jar of Vaseline provides the object through which the daughter finds symbolic relevance, and it is hard not to see a correlation with the Pandora myth here and thus a link to the daughter's initial transgressive acts in "Satan Says." Yet unlike in "The Glass," the jar in "One Secret Thing" does not produce sublime imagery; rather the effect is to create emotional distance, even disdain. The daughter says:

The secret was
how deeply I did not want to touch
inside her, and how much the act
was an act of escape, my last chance
to free myself.

In the remaining poems of the collection, the mother wanes, eventually slips into a coma, and dies, turning into "a thing of bone, / marking where she had been" in "Last Hour" (91). These final poems express the expected rage, grief, and loss and the breakdown of the mourner's worldview. In "To See My Mother" (93), this is symbolized by the mother's devolution ("Embryo, zygote, blastocele, atom, / my mother's dying was like an end / of life on earth"). It is interesting that, in comparison to the treatment of the father's death, the mother's passing receives relatively scant attention and is not nearly so filled with emotional drama. What can be said about the mother's death in context is that, despite the frequent allusions to classical mythology and the Bible, the register of *One Secret Thing* is surprisingly reserved, particularly for a poet as dramatically inclined as Olds. Even in "Nereid Elegy" (97), the final poem of the collection, when the mother's death is "like the death of a god," the language reflects a measure of control and even objectivity. Partly, perhaps, this tonal reserve comes from the evident relief that the character expresses in the final pages; the last line of *One Secret Thing* explains that this new world of the dead gods is like "the birth of an exhausted holiday."

Poems of Motherhood

Sharon Olds is also a mother herself. A significant number of her poems portray children, ostensibly the daughter's children, and these usually reify a central theme of parental trepidation. Denotatively motherhood in the poems describes the pedestrian, everyday tasks of family life—changing, cleaning, succoring, and soothing the minor, incidental traumas of childhood. Thematically Olds's poems of motherhood revolve around four universals: the healing power of motherhood; fear for the safety of all children; the burgeoning sexuality of children; and the inherent, subsumed violence of male children. As is her style, Olds organizes her individual poems into chapters that create a linear narrative out of lyrical vignettes and anecdotes.

When the daughter speaks about her own experiences as a mother, she usually illustrates another central theme: the danger of the outside world for the young. "For and against Knowledge" (*BTS* 90) is one such, although the subject is at first glance unlikely. The poem ostensibly elegizes Christa McAuliffe, one of the astronauts killed in the 1986 space shuttle *Challenger* explosion. McAuliffe, a high school social studies teacher and the first educator chosen for a space mission, was thirty-seven at the time of her death.[1] In the wake of the tragedy, she and the other astronauts became heroes to a nation in mourning. She was posthumously awarded the Congressional Space Medal of Honor. Olds's elegy avoids the obvious connotations of national tragedy to focus on a more personal connection with the woman the poet imagines. She envisions McAuliffe in the physical situation of liftoff, "strapped in, / tilted back, so her back was toward / the planet she was leaving," and then, the effect on the spirit: "did she / weep with excitement in the roar, and in / the lens of a tear glimpse for an instant / a disc of fire?" The poem then turns toward the sphere of domesticity and motherhood, and the poet imagines her own daughter in the space shuttle, imagines how it would feel to be experience the death of a child. The speaker realizes she would worry about the actual manner of her daughter's death ("was she / torn apart, was she burned") as the visceral connection between mother and child manifests in the speaker's imagination. Olds's poems often illustrate an obsessive concern with the situations of children, particularly her own offspring, to such an extent that even a national tragedy becomes fodder for the expression of motherhood. Yet again, however, the poem turns and this time becomes distinctly philosophical, wondering about the metaphysics of the soul: "I have never understood the spirit, / all I know is the shape it takes, / the wavering flame of flesh." The metaphorization of fire in this instance implies not only the manner of the astronaut's death but the evangelical notion of the spirit as a flame. In the final turn, the daughter wishes she could pull the shuttle backward out of the air and pull the astronauts out "like fresh-born creatures . . . family by family" and send them away, safe. As the title indicates, Olds is balancing the desires of the daughters of the world to go forth and find adventure and her desire to see them home safe with their families.

In the same vein, "May 1968" (*TW* 39) dramatizes a mass antiwar protest in New York City. This is the year of the Tet Offensive and, while the poem does not name the conflict per se, the scenario is the social unrest associated with Vietnam War protests. In the context of the poem, the conflict in the streets reflects the great spheres of human violence that menace mothers and children. Almost cinematically New York City looms above the daughter as she lies down on the pavement in protest, and suddenly the city, ostensibly the site of commerce and progress, is gigantic, threatening, and provocative. At its highest point, the sky between the buildings "turned deep blue and then / ashy, colorless." All human society is adversarial at this moment, as is all existence, signified by the empty sky. Such a scene implies an existential universe, one in which the daughter must make her own moral choices without guidance from forces outside herself, and this drives the pregnant daughter to the realization of a greater obligation: the child she carries. From this point forward, the narrative implies, the daughter will put her child before all else, even the most potent causes of the day, and abandon politics and the world for parenthood. In some respects "May 1968" stands opposite Olds's other ars poetica poem that uses parenting as a central vehicle for neglect and abuse, "I Go Back to May 1937." Thirty-one years after her own parents begin their disastrous relationship, the daughter takes on the mantle of parenthood and embraces self-abandonment in a way that her own parents did not. Her declaration becomes even more potent as she abandons the cultural turbulence associated with the Baby Boomers; in "May 1968," the daughter retreats from the defining milieu of her generation and into the private world of the family. "May 1968" pays homage to the civil disobedience that characterized the student protests of the time, and the poem's final meaning is somewhat ambivalent: is the speaker of the poem absolving herself of her obligations to humanity, or is she turning selfishly to her own secure homestead? Perhaps the poem is both a significant portrait of American family life amid geopolitical turmoil and a dramatization of the choices conscientious people must make between home and country.

It should be remembered that Olds herself embodies the spirit of protest from which her poetic persona retreats. In the fall of 2005, First Lady Laura Bush invited a number of prominent poets—including Rita Dove, Philip Levine, and Stanley Kunitz—to a White House poetry reading scheduled on the same day as a protest march against Operation Iraqi Freedom. In response Olds published the controversial "Open Letter to Laura Bush" in the *Nation*.

Olds began her letter by declining the First Lady's "kind invitation" at the same time that she acknowledged that "the idea of speaking at a festival attended by 85,000 people is inspiring!" Rather than immediately turning to her reasons for the decline, Olds then recounted her experiences working with disabled poets "who, in their humor, courage and wisdom, become our teachers." The implication is that literature should be an act of humanity, communication, and learning and that a poet's ultimate purpose is solace. Through her work with the severely disabled, Olds has found "the human drive for creation, self-expression, accuracy, honesty and wit—and the importance of writing, which celebrates the value of each person's unique story and song." She did not explicitly state her purpose here, instead choosing to make her point through implication: compassion is her reason for writing. Although Olds again remarked about the thrilling prospect of the festival, she returned to the purpose of her letter. While missing the possibility of further outreach and the opportunity to express her objections to the Iraq war, "I could not face the idea of breaking bread with you," she wrote. "I knew that if I sat down to eat with you, it would feel to me as if I were condoning what I see to be the wild, highhanded actions of the Bush Administration." Furthermore Olds cited the politically volatile practice, associated specifically with the Bush administration, of "extraordinary rendition: flying people to other countries where they will be tortured for us" as another reason to decline Laura Bush's invitation. Her concluding remark is her most poignant and her most pointed: "So many Americans who had felt pride in our country now feel anguish and shame, for the current regime of blood, wounds and fire. I thought of the clean linens at your table, the shining knives and the flames of the candles, and I could not stomach it."

Response to Olds's letter included the expected conservative backlash in the blogosphere, but letters to the editor published in *The Nation* were generally supportive. However, while the event in question was cancelled (a number of other writers also refused to participate), Olds's letter failed to gamer wide public attention, and Laura Bush's National Book Festival continued through her term as First Lady.

As protest art, Olds's open letter is noteworthy because of its genuine respect for the people and politics the author disagrees with; her tonal reserve stands out during an era associated with the 'Culture Wars' in the media between liberal and conservative commentators. Poet and novelist John Burnside, writing for *The Guardian UK,* observes that, "What makes this document powerful is, in part, its stylistic elegance, as it treads the fine line between political protest and the courtesy that any civilised human being owes to others, no matter how reprehensible their actions. Its effectiveness is enhanced, however, by the trust that a famously rigorous poet inspires; by the authority of one whose main pursuit is not money or fame but artistic integrity."[2] It is interesting to note that Olds has not yet written poetry that deals specifically with the conflicts in Iraq or Afghanistan, but eventually her poems in *One Secret Thing* (2008) tum toward the subject of war and the damage it inflicts upon individuals.

An example of Olds's first universal—the healing love of motherhood—can be seen in "History of Medicine" (*TW* 46), in which the daughter recalls fighting for her child's well-being with bitter remedies. "I fondly remember even Benylin, / Robitussin, Actifed, / Tedral, erythromycin, / penicillin." Once again the incidental corporate accoutrements of American life are reverenced through the act of human contact; however, unlike the earlier example of "One Secret Thing" in the chapter, "History of Medicine" brings commercialized, industrialized America happily into the family sphere. The poem also provides an unusual memory for the daughter in which she is happy: "I can hear my voice, / calm and cheerful." Motherhood affords the daughter a chance to reshape the family dynamic that has wounded her in the past, and she envisions herself as "a young woman with an orderly array of / bottles behind her." In this new role "she is struggling to be good, to be healed."

This topos of the healing mother—healer and protector, as well as healed and enlivened woman-child—is found throughout part 3 of *The Wellspring.* In "First Birth" (43), the daughter expresses the newness of young motherhood: "Each thing / I did, then, I did for the first / time, touched the flesh of our flesh." The next poem in the sequence, "Her First Week" (44), details the fragile nature of the infant ("I was afraid of her neck, once I almost / thought I heard it quietly snap . . . as if the history / of the vertebrate had been placed in my hands"). In "Bathing the Newborn" (45), the speaker recognizes the "almost fearful love" she felt as she soothed her son's instinctive fear of the water during baths; she remembers feeling "the fear / leaving their bodies" from the surety of her maternal nearness. At that moment her son "looked at me in wonder." Once again Olds pays homage to the deific power of the parent, but this time from the parent's point of view looking down on a grateful child.

Boys and Girls

Nevertheless, despite her overarching tenderness, the daughter makes a number of objective observations about the character of the son, namely his natural, childlike propensity for violence, implicating the male gender in the behavior of aggression. In poems such as "Milk-Bubble Ruins" (48) and its companion, "Socks" (49), she has noted the child's destructive propensities without editorial comment. In a typical childhood pastime in "Milk-Bubble Ruins," he blows down his straw into a glass of milk, creating (in Olds's typically virtuoso imagery) "multicellular clouds" that he then proceeds to "pop and dissolve," breaking "each small room of milk." This willingness, eagerness even, to destroy his own creation paints a complicated gestalt of developing masculinity. In "Socks," a poem ostensibly about the simple act of dressing, the daughter promises to play "Ninja Death" (which could refer to any number of games aimed at children during the 1980s and '90s) if the child will throw out a pair of torn socks. His reward is to play a death-game with his mother in which the dice determines "how we will fight" using maces and chains. Similarly "Good Will" (54) records the child's inherent energy and destructiveness as testified by the state of his Lee jeans: ingrained with dirt so they are "worked as a palimpsest," the knees are "exploded . . . the frail, torn, / blue knee open, singing of the boy." In "Solo" (65), recalling a time years later, the daughter listens as her adolescent son leaves their apartment on the way to karate lessons. She hears him "joggle the old elevator button and then / kick it with a flying kick." As if to offset this random outburst of aggression, he sings a few notes of a "Mass or the end of man's childhood." This motion from childish imagination to role-playing to active aggression portrays the stages of the male as he ages into adulthood. Olds—who always inveighs for peace and compassion—is uncharacteristically objective in these poems of gendered violence; it is possible that she wants the scenarios to speak for themselves with her usual acceptance of biological action.

Olds's daughter, on the other hand, is linked to images of reproduction, impending sexuality, and motherhood. "Twelve Years Old" (51) is one of the most overt statements of this kind. As with many of Olds's poems about children, the verse is predicated upon observation. She observes the first hints of adolescence in the child, the "flesh more liquid," "her joints gently rocking her body," and "the front of her / torso smooth, symmetrical, / but her buttocks begin to flash their signals." She dives into the pool "crowded with college boys," and the poet cannot help expressing her own awareness of sexual desire—which she recognizes will soon be a force in her child's life. With a typically unsettling metaphor for sexual penetration, the poet describes as the child "enters the water with the charged thrust of her / knife into the chicken in a dream when she is really hungry." Again observation is essentially objective and biology is an accepted fact, but the imagery suggests waiting desire and ever-present danger. Compare this evocation with that of the son in "Solo": rather than receiving karate lessons, the female child must dive into liquid menace and hope for the best.

Two companion poems from *The Dead and the Living*—"Size and Sheer Will" (69) and "For My Daughter" (65)—carry the children's collective development into their distinct futures. Most notable about the pairing are the respective gender roles the children inhabit: the male child longs to be sixteen, the age when American adolescents can legally drive and thus become free and powerful; and the female child can look forward to a future when she becomes pregnant. This dichotomy reflects a traditional American mindset that perceives women as child-bearers and men as adventurers. In "Size and Sheer Will," the male child is growing, thrusting into new life, so that his pajamas have "split like a sheath." His natural action is vigorous assertion, even to the point of necessary, biologically driven expansion. He is "growing / as fast as he can . . . like a plant in the dark with a single / light above it, or a sailor under / tons of green water, longing . . . for his rightful life." It is an interesting comment considering the cautionary nature of burgeoning maturity in men (that they become killers) in "Rite of Passage" (66), the following poem about the male child. And yet, as is often the case when Olds considers the gendered subject and sexuality, the "rightful life" of the male child is one filled with machines and speed.

Conversely "For My Daughter" appears to celebrate the onset of puberty as a conduit to familial obligation. Images in the poem suggest the loss of virginity and phallic violence but finally sexual freedom. Sexual autonomy comes with a price to the body; the "center" of the girl's body is metaphorically torn open by the loss of virginity, as "a woman will rip the / seam of her skirt so she can run." Interestingly the prescient narrator sees in her child's future a similar familiar relationship to her own. She wishes to pass on the health and fidelity of her own marriage to her own child—and this bountiful transference begins with sex. These are "versions of the story / that changes in the telling, the story of the river" that is the elixir of life. Olds also utilizes a familiar image, the river that is never the same twice because of its constant flowing, in a new configuration: in "For My Daughter," the future is similarly constantly in motion. As with the poems of sexual liberation in which sex represents freedom from the oppressive mother, the daughter's child also achieves the ability to tear loose the seams that constrain her and "run" by achieving the fecundity of womanhood. Yet the child's role is essentially that of a wife and mother, an inherently sexual being; here again sex is the receptacle of pleasure and of the continuation of family. Eventually, however, these declarations about marriage prove ironic in Olds's Pulitzer Prize–winning *Stag's Leap*, in which sexual liberation is actually a divisive, destructive force in the relationship between a husband and wife.

A similar dichotomy of gender roles exists in *The Wellspring* in a trio of linked poems, "Physics" (66), "My Son the Man" (67), and "First Formal" (68). All three deal with the ceremonial sundering of the parent/child bond in late adolescence, and each deals with the daughter's sense of mourning afterward. "I have lived as my daughter's mother / the way I had lived as my mother's daughter," she says in "Physics" (a poem in which her daughter works in a field of science still dominated by men); "I have not been born yet." This sense of incompleteness contradicts earlier observations of motherhood in the poetry and seems to symbolize a number of conflicts: mother/daughter, as the child supersedes the adult; personal/cultural, as the daughter realizes that she still carries the ideals of femininity from past generations; and motherhood/adolescence, the female child's intellectual growth that generates an independence from the daughter and a reckoning of the daughter's own limitations. Most interesting, however, are the alternating gendered descriptions of the two children. For the son, the body is the site of startling trickery, even magic, full of the strength and energy of masculinity: "Suddenly his shoulders get a lot wider, / the way Houdini would expand his body" ("My Son the Man"). And the daughter is forced to confront this new strength even as she wants to deny childhood's end:

> I cannot imagine him
> no longer a child, and I know I must get ready,
> get over my fear of men now my son
> is going to be one.

For the male child, the agon is created by a need to escape from his mother's influence, a move that, in the narrator's perception, is accompanied by a gentle pandering: he eyes her "the way Houdini studied a box" to devise an escape, and then he smiles and allows himself to be manacled. Once again the narrator is the weaker entity in relation to a male family member. She is the trap from which her son will somewhat mysteriously escape using his wit and burgeoning strength. In contrast the female child in "First Formal," the last poem in the trio, is oddly purified, sexualized, and then infantilized; she "rises" from her strapless dress, "flesh like a soul half out of a body," as if "her body might pour up out of the bodice," and yet "she looks / hatched this moment." The narrator's association is one not of escape but of her in her crib, "so slight, looking worn out from her journey" and gazing at her parents "in dubious willingness."

Part 3 of *The Dead and the Living,* aptly titled "The Children," comprises twenty paired poems that alternate between male and female subjects as if to offer entwined gender perspectives. The section moves from the outer world, with its complicated adult relationships and perilous sexuality, into the private sphere of the family. The progression of *The Dead and the Living* as a whole is from the macrocosm of the world stage through the conduit of the public sphere and into the microcosm of the family.

"Exclusive" (61), dedicated to Olds's daughter, deals with the intense feelings associated with maternal love and, at the same time, with the recognition that there are limits even to the life-giving authority of the mother. Formally "Exclusive" develops much like an elegy, beginning with a portrait of the subject, then moving to a profession of the speaker's love for the subject, and finally arriving at acceptance of the inevitability of loss. And in a sense the poem is an elegy, for the loss of the total, perfect, ideological love for her child. As is so often the case with Olds's imagery, the child is portrayed with startling biological descriptors; she has "empurpled lips, swollen in the sun / and smooth as the inner lips of a shell"; her skin is "biscuit-gold" and "faintly pitted"; her hair is "serious knotted twine." Such a distinctive vision reflects the daughter's sudden new conception, and certain descriptions ("empurpled lips") seems to describe a newborn infant. Then, following the close observation of her child, the speaker is overcome with the intensity of her emotion and claims, "I have loved you instead of anyone else," which leads her to the realization that "I had learned the love of other lips." Love of others in the world comes from loving those closest to the speaker; the intensity of her love for her daughter forces her out into the world and to the realization the even devotion has limits. In its final analysis, "Exclusive" is a poem about the imperfect beauty of love.

The companion poem is a rather odd, arguably uncouth celebration of the male child's future potency. "Six-Year-Old Boy" (61) is potentially shocking in its descriptions and references to the child's penis. The narrative is relatively simple, if not usually material for family recollection (the daughter returns from a long car trip at night and allows her drowsing child son to urinate upon the lawn). As the car pulls into the drive, she turns to look into the backseat only to find that her son's "hard-on lifts his pajamas like the / earth above the shoot of a bulb." She then rouses the child and watches as he sleepily urinates. Such indelicate intimacy is, no doubt, a perfect example of how Olds's poetry alienates a great many readers, as taboos of decency and childhood are uncomfortably, even egregiously transgressed. Olds's focus is repeatedly on the biological processes of her son, present and future—an uncomfortable closeness in this narrative. However, as is always the case, the motivation behind her unstinting examination of bodies is to discover the archetypal themes—true metanarratives—symbolized and foreshadowed by biology, that which is the vehicle of the spirit and intimately tied to the spirit's well-being. In this context the boy's penis will metaphorically take him forward "into his life." At present he is a child, under the command of his simple biological needs; in the future, like the bulb his prepubescent erection portends, he will be a source of reproduction and thus life.

The penis, so often a symbol of masculine hedonism, pornography, violence, and oppression, also represents fecundity and promise in Olds's poetry. While she is aware of male violence, the effect of the phallus is generally positive, as are descriptions of sex in general. As with "Six-Year-Old Boy," any sense of shame is assuaged by the acceptance of the human and surprisingly affirmative scrutiny of biology, as opposed to a forensic or aestheric approach. The counterpart to the penis, naturally, is the human egg in the female child's body. "Eggs," the poem which follows "Six-Year-Old-Boy," is a poem about the fertility of the poet's young daughter. For Olds the greatest potential for the child is what she means for future generations. Yet, in the first line of the poem, the child has moved away from the beauty of reproduction—"My daughter has turned against eggs." Olds does well with the hook into the action and, like any good dramatic opening, the line is meant to arouse curiosity through its strangeness. "Eggs" moves from a description of the young girl as a cook—innocent of both the importance and the danger of life-giving—to an elder child disgusted by cooking's complications. Fertility's devolution is symbolized by the cooking process itself, an analog to the gestation of the fetus, which the child will abandon: "It gets on her hands, it's slimy, and it's hard / to get all the little things out." Nevertheless the inevitable time of fecundity is coming. The child is nine years old, the narrator relates: "It is getting / too close. Next birthday she's ten and then / it's open season." With the onset of puberty, men will become hunters, and the daughter's maternal fears manifest in a series of metaphors for fertility and the body. "No telling when / the bright, crimson dot" of menstruation will appear, an image Olds links to fertilized chicken eggs. Yet rather than a denunciation of the dangers of adult sexuality, "Eggs" affirms the life-giving power of women and encourages them to accept this power; the alternative—to "quit eggs"—leaves one as emotionally distraught as the child is at the end of the poem. In the final evaluation, "Eggs" is a call to action. Always woven into Olds's domestic tapestries are the issues that women face, in this instance in the form of a call to evaluate women's roles in the domestic sphere. It would be too simple to suggest that Olds wants a return to the "barefoot and pregnant" stereotype of the homebound housewife pre–second wave feminism; the poem does not support this. But Olds does appear to suggest that separation from the life-giving powers of the body is also spiritual and thus doubly painful.

Part 3 of *The Wellspring*

The third part of *The Wellspring* is focused specifically on the firstborn female child and the poet's self-identification as a mother. The timeframe of the sequence covers her children's growth from infancy to adolescence. Throughout she expresses the now familiar topos of nonmaternal femininity as incomplete and motherhood as the anodyne. "I felt as if / I was nothing, no one," the poet says of her life before motherhood in "First Birth" (43). She then contrasts this alienation to the fulfillment of family, a statement that expresses the essential function of family life: "I was everything to her," the poet says of her first child, and then to give voice to the equilibrium that comes from this realization, she says, "I was hers." Her child was the wellspring of the daughter's new self-esteem. A wellspring, in the strictly denotative sense, is the source of a spring or stream, an original and bountiful source of inexhaustible supply. The implication is clear that the daughter has found a sustaining, much-needed passion that provides perspective to the turbulence almost fanatically memorialized in her other poems of childhood and adolescence. At the same time, the intensity of the emotion suggests a codependent psyche, a mother whose identity is predicated upon her children's unwavering attention.

If there is a final image to consider in Olds's mother poems, it is the broken cow butter dish in "Lament" (55), a self-revelatory reflection about the nature of motherhood on the verge of an empty nest. Her children are nearly grown and in the home less and less. Realizing this, the poet relates herself to a kitchen item that has been broken "like a mercy killing." She spends her time cradling the dish almost as if it were an infant, kisses "her mild / dumb forehead," observes the nearly sexual contours of the porcelain figure's interior, and yet reiterates the deific power of the parent, "the way God might have sat on the bank / shaping the clay." The poet laments the literal destruction of the dish, which even "on the hottest day" would keep butter cool; symbolically, accidentally, she also mourns her own connection to motherhood, which was smashed at some indeterminate but nearby point in time, and the symbolic death of dedicated, protective maternity. Olds is a poet dedicated to elegy, and she is a family oriented. These two elements converge in "Lament." The poem seems like a fitting finale to her complex portrait of motherhood.

CHAPTER 5

Love, Good Sex, Bad Sex, Sex and Marriage, Divorce

Olds's poetic voice, virtually always female, is unapologetic in its celebration of the sexual act. Olds enjoys taking readers into the experience—into the visceral, hedonistic joy of sex, a sensual woman's gratitude afterward, the potential for violence associated with the act, and the emotional disequilibrium that human beings experience before, after, and even during it. Men in her poems are often portrayed as victims of their own biological urges, and yet they are often the saviors of the poems' first-person speaker, who evinces the same demeanor and attitude toward sex throughout Olds's work. Generally receptive and even grateful for their predatory aggression, she responds to them with her own sympathetic compulsion for sex. Alluded to and never entirely forgotten, however, are the victims of violence, particularly, as recounted in "Necking" (*TW* 25), a girl from the speaker's childhood who was raped and killed and who now haunts a number of Olds's poems. By blending so many experiences through the narrator's individual perception, Olds has created a spokeswoman for the multifarious experiences of women in a highly sexualized, often voyeuristic American milieu. For example, in reference to losing her virginity, the narrator of "Animal Music" (*BTS* 6) says:

> It felt like there were an army inside me,
> maybe at the second when the parted walls
> of the Red Sea closed, again, with their shining
> clasping closings.

It is hard not to read the experience as one of essentially religious significance: the narrator utilizes a hyperbolic symbology that celebrates and even privileges male sexuality as a conduit to ecstasy. Images of male aggression ("army inside of me") are yoked to iconic biblical imagery ("the Red Sea closed") in a manner that suggests the enormity of the experience, both physical and spiritual. The body has been split, invaded, and forever changed by the necessary godlike violence of the experience. At the same time, the speaker's psyche has escaped to the Promised Land of future sexual encounters through the blood rite of the first union. This view of sex and sexuality reverses the norms of the confessional aesthetic, which generally expresses visceral disgust for the human body. Sylvia Plath's allegory of first sex, "Bucolics," for example, is a poem of ineffective chivalry, describing the aftermath in pseudoromantic diction as "rueful, most vexed, that tender skin / Should accept so fell a wound."[1] Anne Sexton's "Old Dwarf Heart," a poem about sensual love, opens "When I lie down to love, old dwarf heart shakes her head" as if in disapproval or disgust. The body in Sexton's poem is "the decay we're made of." When she dreams of loving, Sexton's narrator says, "my dreams are of snarling strangers."[2] This is not to suggest that all confessional poets approach sexuality as dire failure—W. D. Snodgrass, for instance, repeatedly beseeches his readers to fight for the joy of love—but human contact in the genre is generally portrayed as painful.

Olds's speaker, on the other hand, approaches sex with enthusiasm and humor. An odd but perfectly apt example is "The Connoisseuse of Slugs," which begins the sequence of poems "The Men" in *The Dead and the Living* (51). A connoisseuse is a female connoisseur. "The Connoisseuse of Slugs" is perhaps Olds's most overt poem of the female gaze, although the enactment is unique and unexpected. Rising slug eyestalks represent the phallus and sexual excitement, and the speaker is a voyeur, peering through the vines into the secret world where sexual arousal takes place. Men's penises are implicitly metaphorized as "the glimmering umber horns / rising like telescopes" from the heads of slugs. Years later the speaker "gasped with pleasure to see that quiet / mystery reenacted" by a naked man. In Olds's portrayal, safety is of prime importance to the act of stimulation. Shy as the delicate animals hiding in the shadows, male sexuality must be coaxed out in private for the magic of nature to take place. Male sexuality, so often associated with aggression and predatory nature, is rendered as a simple, reticent, easily damaged, golden-skinned animal, "gleaming in the dark air, eager and so / trusting you could weep." Virility in this allegory represents nature and the natural process of growth, which is nevertheless a private, cautious, voyeuristic pleasure for the female observer.

In Olds's inner landscape, sex is an act of faith and trust, particularly considering that she is a poet who explicitly deals with violence toward woman (see "The Girl" [*TGC* 14] or "Republican Living Rooms" [*SS* 16] as examples).

Because of this faith in masculine sexuality, she can successfully portray men as vulnerable creatures, counteracting the violence of traditional versions of masculinity. "Poem to My First Lover" (*TDATL* 52) meditates upon the theme of adolescent awkwardness and the sexual act; the girl is "mad with love," while the boy feels "terror" over what he is about to do and the necessary violence of penetration, "deflowering her as you'd gut a fish" or pry an "escargot from its dark shell." This conceit of the girl as sea life, flopping nakedly against his knees as if drawn into a boat, is related back to the boy's terror, yet this is assuaged as the speaker says, "I am in awe of terror that will / waste so much." Her purpose is to take this terror and turn it into a "feast on a platter" through the quasi-sexual diction of "yes, yes, / I accept the gift." The gentle male is finally brought to fruition in the next poem in *The Dead and the Living*, "New Mother" (53), the title of which implies a poem about maternity. However, new motherhood, after the physiological reality of childbirth, is a delicate time for sexuality. The speaker is hyperaware of her biological self—the smell of "fresh milk, sour," the "sex . . . torn easily as cloth" by the birthing process—and of the delicate state of the human organism at this time; implicit is the trauma and natural violence of childbirth and the many vulnerabilities of the new mother. In this context Olds presents a version of nurturing, protective manhood in the form of a nurse

> with the patience of someone who
> finds a wounded animal in the woods
> and stays with it, not leaving its side
> until it is whole, until it can run again.

The relationship between these two, the gentle husband and the appreciative wife, then takes a surprising narrative turn in the next poem in the section, "The Line" (54). When the wife is faced with a biological betrayal by her own body—a "small hard lump," presumably breast cancer—"There was no question of / making love" despite the visceral comfort provided by the husband. The physical act of love is distinctly joyful in Olds's poetry, a conduit to the life-giving process, and the seriousness of the situation is conveyed by its abandonment.

It should be pointed out that Olds does not embrace a worldview of hedonism without consequences. Always she has written with concern for the sanctity of life. "The End" (26), which follows its partner poem, "Miscarriage" (25), dramatizes the alternative to nature's fragile process as the deliberate, violent carelessness of humanity. "The End" is a largely symbolic narrative in which an automobile accident provides a correlative to the abortion process. Both are brutal interruptions of life:

> Cops pulled the bodies out
> bloody as births from the small, smoking
> aperture of the door, laid them
> on the hill, covered them with blankets that soaked
> through.

Overlooking such a scene, the speaker must deal with her own culpability, and the blood that begins to pour down her legs in a visceral response will not be easily removed, just like the memory of abortion will follow, like footprints in blood. Readers, like the speaker, are meant to understand that their rationalization of death (an accident, as no wanted baby is ever aborted) leaves guilty impressions upon their minds. Because we live in a land of plenty with room and sustenance enough for all, even the unwanted, the sexual indulgence that accompanies death must be soaked and scoured "to deglaze the pan / when the feast is over."

"The Solution" (*TGC* 17) is an example of Olds's black humor. The tone of the poem is unusually conversational and polemical. "Finally they got the Singles problem under / control," the speaker says; "they made it scientific." The scientific solution is to pair couples based upon their desires: people who want to touch and hold are paired with those that want to be touched and held; masochists are paired with sadists; and so on. Perhaps the poem's funniest joke is the "Berkeley, California, policeman" who stands under the sign "*Married Adults, Lights Out, Face to Face, Under a / Sheet.*" For some reason this is the only legal position for sex in Berkeley—although Olds may be playing with the irony of stifling sexual conduct in the famously liberal California city. Then "things began to get strange." The designations become increasingly unlikely and impersonal. The "*Love Only—No Sex*" and "*Sex Only—No Love*" queues do well, with "pair after pair walking out / together like wooden animals off a child's ark." Not coincidentally the dangers of hedonism and pornography become more apparent: "*38D or Bigger* was getting unruly, / shouting insults at the line for *8 Inches or / Longer.*" At the same time, "isolated signs" for sexual fetishes are "springing up everywhere." Most alarmingly

> The line
> under I Want to Be Fucked Senseless was so long
> that portable toilets had to be added and a minister
> brought for deaths, births, and marriages on the
> line.

The line continues to grow until it "stretched across the nation in / a huge wide belt like the Milky Way," and this, the poet explains us, is called the "American

Way." Olds's point with this rather unlikely allegory is that, by making sex "scientific," by removing the human connection to the most human of activities, the United States has become a mass Sodom that affects the entire world. Science, in this context, is a synecdoche for the entire sexual revolution and the modern sexual milieu; science is impersonal, objective, voyeuristic, and predicated entirely on the attainment of its objective.

The Wellspring: Part 2

Another prime example of Olds as a poet of endangered but unabashedly sensual women, part 2 of *The Wellspring* contains eleven poems entirely dedicated to sex—the narrator's first negotiations of it, her subsequent longing for it, love as the expression of it, visions of it as a mythical construct, and the eventual culmination of it in motherhood. These five ideals (intimations, longing, love, myth, and motherhood) represent the themes of sexuality generally found in Olds's work. As an individual assemblage of poems, part 2 represents the multiple perspectives of experience in which sex is a "raw mystery I liked" ("First"), a palliative that "stoppers the hole behind the breastbone that is always hungry" ("The Source"), and an initiation "sending me down to be born" ("After Making Love in Winter"). In these poems, as in others about sex, Olds reclaims sexuality as a site of healing and creation as well as danger.

The first poem in the section, "Necking" (25), describes a typical adolescent activity: making out in an automobile, in this cases at a secluded spot that overlooks a "Cyclotron" and "the Rad Lab." This unlikely pairing of situation and location contributes to the meaning of the poem and begins in media res the journey through the chapter. Images of contamination combine with sexually suggestive language to intimate the complex matrix of sexuality and gender history. The narrator is reminded of the "paintbrush tips the watch-girls licked," an allusion to the women who worked in the United States Radium Corporation painting luminous watch faces with paint made from a mixture of glue and radium. The watches were then sold to the United States military. The women, commonly known as "radium girls," were trained by their supervisors to shape the brushes to fine points by wetting them with their lips. In the process the women ingested dangerous radioactive carcinogens, and a number became ill—it is unknown how many died. In the subconscious the paintbrushes equate to phallic symbols implying the hazards of sex (oral sex most obviously), Cold War science (which creates light, a protean motif in the poem), and the nearness of male aggression. Glowing "Arabic numerals on the dashboards," ostensibly composed of the same material that sickened the radium girls, are warning signals subsumed into visceral pleasure as the narrator and her lover "slid slowly / along each other" with surprising placidity. She does recall that "the rape / and murder of our classmate had happened in these hills," reminding herself of the always looming threat of gendered violence, but the poem turns toward a sympathetic evocation of masculine sexuality: "the way they carried / the longing of the species, you could not help but pity them / as they set you on stunned fire." There is something essential and necessary in this longing, and Olds's point seems to be that the species needs the terrible yet wonderful sexual aggression of the male animal to propagate. At the same time, her inclusion of geopolitics should not be overlooked. The radium girls are a synecdoche of massive Cold War science and politics endangering people of all ages and situations, even teenagers involved in the inciting incidents of procreation, the counterforce that creates rather than destroys life. Olds frequently uses this juxtaposition of personal and political situations as a commentary on the era and the human condition.

In the next poem, "First" (27), dangerous sex is juxtaposed to the comparatively earnest and therefore innocent sexual activities in "Necking." "First," conversely, is about hedonistic sex. In a sulphur bath, at night, after many drinks, the narrator performs oral sex on a man for the first time. The man is "a writer, married, a father, widowed, / remarried, separated, unreadable." In other words the daughter does not know him, nor does she really care. His import is his relationship to sex and sexual aggression. As is typical Olds's narrator responds with a surprising sympathy for the sexually forceful male. "I had not heard / of this [oral sex], I was moved by his innocence and daring," she says, even as he rises from the water and presents her with "his body to suck." In response she infantilizes herself—"I went to him like a baby who's been crying / for hours for milk"—before they both collapse, and the daughter admits, "*I've never done that before.*" Rather than demonstrating any tenderness, gratitude, or affection, the man responds with objectifying psychological violence:

> His eyes not visible
> to me, his voice muffled, he said, *You've been*
> *sucking cock since you were fourteen*,
> and fell asleep.

The narrator stays beside the man in the hot tub "so he wouldn't go under" (tellingly "he snored like my father"), rocking and thinking about what he had said. She takes his insult as an "unmeant / gift . . . I was good at this / raw mystery I liked." Sex is a reward worth the price. The male's aggressive, insensitive, misogynistic sexuality is legitimized through the narrator's frank enjoyment of the act.

Psychological portraiture in this instance could follow several lines of explication. On the one hand, the narrator has once again tellingly exposed her

Electra complex and her need to appease abusive men. She is subject to male desire and self-infantilizing. The feminine is subjugated, exploited even, at the same time that her self-description is more appropriate to a mother. Equality in the sexual arena is willingly, almost aggressively, dissolved by the person who should defend it. On the other hand, the narrator can be read as sexually empowered, engaging in an encounter as a matter of personal exploration. Or it could be that these two philosophical poles are intertwined.

"Adolescence" (29), the next poem in the sequence, expounds on this same contradictory blend of gender roles and sexuality. As with "Necking" and "First," the setting reflects the degradation of the persona, "the bathroom of that seedy hotel / in San Francisco, where my boyfriend would take me," a situation that seems more adult than adolescent.

> I had never seen a bathroom like that—
> no curtains, no towels, no mirror, just
> a sink green with grime and a toilet
> yellow and rust-colored—like something in a science experiment,
> growing the plague in bowls.
> Sex was still a crime, then.

Linking sex to a devolving world of sought-after degradation, even humiliation, is a common theme. At the same time, when she is being humorous, Olds tends toward the grotesque and the slapstick to critique contemporary sexual morality. The diaphragm she "decorates . . . like a cake" with spermicide slips from her fingers and flies across the room. Sex and the individual are reduced to their most undignified selves, reflecting the innate indignity in the sexual act itself. Eros has been elided by the medical apparatus that hampers procreation, the healthy endpoint of sex. Nevertheless by the end of the poem, the speaker recollects "kneeling" like a penitent and crawling for her sprung diaphragm as if "reaching for my life." It is a paradoxical ending to a pointed critique of the forces that drive young people, posing more questions than it answers—is the persona reaching for sexual fulfillment? Would this fulfillment give her life meaning? Or is she straining for escape from the underworld? At the same time, is this simply an admission of an undeniable sex drive? In poems of this nature, Olds has written from the perspective, and with the articulateness, of a mature adult reflecting on a time of life now safely past. Looking back at the sexual revolution, the poems are a fusion of critique and celebration. Sexuality in her characters' lives is represented without themes of regret, yet there are the unmistakable caveats to each of her sexualized scenarios, particularly when associated with the radicalism apparent in 1960s and 1970s, a period when Olds would have been in her twenties and early thirties. Sexuality became political during this time, a force to express rebellion and liberation. Now, from her position as mature poet, Olds dramatizes these changes through humorous cautionary tales.

However, the next three poems in part 2 of *The Wellspring*—"Early Images of Heaven," "Celibacy at Twenty," and "The Source"—counteract the cautionary ethos of the first three by celebrating lust, even if there is an emotional cost. In "Early Images of Heaven" (30), the fourth poem of the section, she says boldly that penises are "the way I would have designed them if I had / invented them." She marvels about their physical properties, their "suppleness," "the way the head barely fits in the throat," and even the hair that lifts "delicate / and free." Such a frank admission is empowering as it celebrates the phallus as an object of desire. The female speaker is egalitarian (she wonders if the penis were made for her pleasure or for his), but she is clearly the connoisseur, and the penis is personified and the willing recipient of her attention. The fact that Olds privileges sex and explicates it from the feminist point of view is worthy of note in this context. Gone are any hints of awkwardness, shame, embarrassment, or abuse. Women, Olds implicitly argues, need not be ashamed of their sensual selves. Sex is a necessary, beneficial biological urge, and by the end of the poem, her desire, as the title implies, has religious overtones befitting sexuality's importance to life. Yet as is virtually always the case, the poem turns toward patriarchy, and the experience is "like God / the Father all around me." Taken as an individual poem, the reference is religious iconography juxtaposed to the human act of procreation. Viewed as part of Olds's larger body of work, however, the final statement is familiar territory: the power of the father figure surrounds all aspects of life, even the intimate moments. If there is a method of rebellion, it is the celebration of life-giving power, that which the father does not have, for which sex is a synecdoche.

"Celibacy at Twenty" (31) speaks directly to the speaker's powerful, almost compulsive sexual drive: "if I turned a corner too / fast" after going too long without sex, she says, "I would almost come." Such exaggerated statements illustrate Olds's surprising humor, an aspect of her poetry that is often lost among her more serious works. The poem notes the reason for this obsessive desire is the emotional connection it enables: "soon there were the last kisses, and I / felt I stood outside of life." "The Source" (33) makes plain that the source of this pleasure is the male body. Once again sex is described as a means to fill an emotional void:

> to grasp that band of muscle on the male
> haunch and help guide the massed
> heavy nerve down my throat until it

> stoppers the hole behind the breastbone that is always hungry,
> then I feel complete.

Olds tends toward heavy-handed metaphors, particularly when the vehicle is sexuality, and "The Source" ends on the conceit of the human race "swimming by the cinerous / millions" until they unite through sex and achieve a momentary respite, a "pure calm, as if each one of us is whole." Sex is likened to death, an allusion to *la petite mort* but also an idea consistent with Olds's other abstractions of danger in poetry and society.

The poem that follows is a stylistic rarity for Olds, redefining the confessional I and challenging the notion of the subject. "Making Love" (35) is written in the second person, implicating the reader in what appears, at first, to be a "morning after" scenario. The scene follows, not coincidentally, the vast orgiastic bath that culminates "The Source." "You wake up, and you do not know / where you are," the speaker directly addresses the reader, "or who you are / or what you are." Once again Olds is writing into the sexual zeitgeist of contemporary American morality. She presumes a familiarity on the part of the reader with the ethos of "hook-up" culture and uses this to argue about its dangers, psychological and literal. The loss of identity enunciated in the opening lines implies the psychological effect of anonymous sexual union. Then the *you* of the poem realizes that it is actually late in the day, "the last light of the evening / coming up the panes," and this further adds to the confusion of the scene. "You" note the disarray in the room, the clothes strewn in strange places, and realize that the encounter, whatever happened there, is lost to memory. The encounter has submerged into the subconscious, where "it stands behind your mind, like a mountain, at night"—and suddenly the scenario seems much more like a date rape, in which "you cannot remember, everything is changed." What has happened is not "making love" at all; the title is meant as irony of the darkest, noncomedic kind. Body images are rendered almost as carnage that mirrors the psychological damage done by the rapist. It makes sense, suddenly, for the second person indicative as a mode of communication to the reader: Olds has put the reader in the place of the victim. Whatever has happened has vanished from the sunlit world but lingers in the mind until the repressed memory is triggered, apropos of nothing, and rises from the depths of the subconscious. The speaker warns the reader, "you'll / see his mouth where it was and feel it and the / large double star of your two bodies." The world changes around the "you" of the poem who is suddenly, literally, both "like the one in the crib" and "everyone," even as the memory resubmerges into the subconscious.

Part of Olds's power as a commentator upon contemporary mores is her response to issues of violence and sexuality; namely she refuses to inveigh against the sexual politics of an era or to demonize the male gender. She is not, in other words, interested in battling the patriarchy solely for the sake of polemics or the political cause of feminism. She responds to the dreadfulness of the scenario in "Making Love" with its companion poem, "I Love It When" (36), a poem that simply (perhaps too simply) celebrates sexual intercourse. Olds has returned to the first person here yet speaks directly to the reader as, once again, "you"—"I love it when you roll over / and lie on me in the night." The images in "I Love It When" strain metaphorically to describe the intense visceral experience of the sex act ("I love to feel you grow and grow be- / tween my legs like a plant in fast motion"), and the ending of the poem suggests a simplified, almost adolescent expression of lust rather than a mature statement. But the purpose of the poem can be most readily understood as an anodyne to the trauma of the previous poem about rape. In this way Olds readily acknowledges the different poles of female sexual experience while at the same time refusing to demonize all men.

Other poems in the section follow these general paradigms of dangerous sex ("The Dragons") and tender monogamous sex ("After Making Love in Winter") until the final entry in the section, "May 1968," which is a counterstatement to Olds's well-known "I Go Back to May 1937." Olds's general motion in this section of *The Wellspring* is toward healing personal, and thus social, wounds—sexual tensions foremost among these.

"The Dragons" (37) is largely without a literary progenitor and is difficult to explicate using the ordinary tools of close reading. As a commentary on contemporary morals and an allegory of human sexual cupidity, the poem is resonant, but the strangeness of its scenario offsets any too worldly interpretation. Olds has evoked the mythology of sexual union; the dragons are mythical beasts, and yet they seem to follow the primitive but familiar instincts of the animal kingdom. Violence and sex are wound into the same act. Olds has deliberately stretched the possibilities of poetry—particularly from the perspective of the confessional mode that privileges the literalness of the retelling—into imaginative confabulation, perhaps the proper place for sex.

The Dead and the Living: Good Sex

In other instances, as discussed above, Olds distinctly connects the sex to love, and by and large the ostensible argument running through much of her poetry is that spiritual union is the overarching achievement of the sexual union. For instance the character of the daughter firmly reemerges in "Poem to My Husband from My Father's Daughter" (*TDATL* 56), a poem in which she reckons with the inhumanity, the genetics of psychic danger, passed down to her from the father. "I see I am / my father as a woman," she says; "you can / see his hair springing from my head like / oil from the ground." It is an odd simile. The most immediate associations with oil are its darkness, its noxious viscosity, and its ability to coat and pollute. Its origin in death and ancient prehistory (the fact that it is the eons-old product of the breaking down of extinct biological matter) also should not be overlooked. "Poem to My Husband" is a poem about evolution from this creature with the black ichor of family dysfunction into a women set free by the sanctity of sex. It is obvious that the daughter recognizes how her past relationship with the father now affects her relationship with her husband. And in this scenario it is the husband who is the hero. "You flood your seed in his [the father's] / life as in me," the daughter apostrophizes the husband; "you entrust your children to that / man as a mother." She likens herself to a lion ready to be tamed by the husband. The lion's threat is distinctly sexual (her "great tongue" running along his skin) in the discourse of the poem, until it ends with an ecstatic exchange of sexual love. The focus is on the husband ("as you enter / ecstasy," she says to him, describing his reaction to the sexual act) and the effect their lovemaking is a panacea to the pollution of the father. "Poem to My Husband from My Father's Daughter" is an answer to "The Fear of Oneself" (55), which immediately precedes it. Fear is negated by the faithful act of lovemaking.

The next poem in the sequence, "Sex without Love" (57), however, takes an almost clinical view of pornographic actors, asking the question, "How do they do it, the ones who make love / without love?" The speaker answers that

> These are the true religious,
> the purists, the pros, the ones who will not
> accept a false Messiah, love the
> priest instead of the God.

These lovers understand their own aloneness, their own biological reality, so they do not "mistake the lover for their own pleasure." One of Olds's many strengths as a poet is her ability to step outside the romantic tradition of the individual as arbiter of experience and embrace the cultural effects of being within an existential universe. This is one such example. It is a cold reality, she argues in "Sex without Love," but for the loveless lover, the sexual act is a "single body alone in the universe / against its own best time." Yet as is so often the case in Olds's collections, the next poem, which is also the concluding poem in the section, creates an implicit argument for the spiritual value of physical love while at the same time warning against complete surrender to pleasures of the flesh.

"Ecstasy" (58), as the title suggests, expresses sexual pleasure. It is an unusual poem for Olds in that it allows a collage of natural images to carry the tenor of sexual intimacy into an almost religious rapture. "Black rocks," "patches of snow," "black mountains rising from the hills" reify the immense emotional experience of three days of sexual union; both participants are borne up in a version of romantic sublimity. "One huge / cloud with scalloped edges of blazing / evening light" symbolizes the passage to the ideal. The cloud's implications of barely revealed energy speak to the numinous possibilities of physical sensation. Olds seldom lets the images carry such weight in her poetry, and it is noteworthy here that she allows her narration to become metaphysical. Sex, the flesh, is catalyst for the mystical experience, but such an elevation (because ascent is the overriding metaphor) comes with a surprising danger. Images of rocks, mountains, lakes are all colored black, and the eventual destination is a "place from which no one has ever come back." The poem should be read as a caveat in this regard: such complete submission to the flesh, while it produces sensual joy, can be fatal. As elsewhere in her poetry, Olds suggests here that the carnival of desire must not become consuming, no matter how wondrous the experience.

Despite these qualified celebrations of sexuality, the putative partner, her husband, is a relatively rarity in the poetry. He is first seen early on in *Satan Says* in the companion poems "Feared Drowned" (28) and "Station" (29), both of which utilize motifs of distance and water to symbolize an otherwise unvoiced conundrum of married life. "Feared Drowned" is a poem on the theme of perceived absence and emotional distance. Swimming in the ocean, the husband goes missing among the other swimmers; the speaker wears her "towel / like a widow's shawl." When he does return,

> Coming closer, he turns out
> to be you—or nearly.
> Once you lose someone it is never exactly
> the same person who comes back.

He seems to draw away from her even as he comes near. Like other artists of the postmodern era, Olds sums up the disconnectedness, even loneliness, of individuals in American life. In her particular scenario, the ocean (the perennial symbol of both life and death), nearly obliterates her husband; his eventual reemergence produces, not the original, but a simulacra of the powerful male, a new iteration of the ruling individual who has been involved in a typical masculine pursuit of energy and exercise. The final meaning of this situation is left ambiguous in the poem: has the poet described the natural fear of separation, be it from natural or spiritual forces, or has she described a scenario in which any separation creates a small but notable difference?

"Station" draws out this same distance in terms that are less alarming in regard to the physical environment but more unsettling in terms of psychological portraiture. "Coming in off the dock after writing," the poet says, "I . . . saw your long grandee face" illuminated in a window of the house. From the outset in her perception, the husband holds an almost divine dignity, and the speaker must undergo his scrutiny, no matter how accidentally, as she returns from her own vocation on the water much as he returned from his own exertion in the previous poem. A generally unlikely location for a writer to do her work, the dock symbolizes the extension of the poet into elemental life. And yet the result is not renewal or rebirth but a questionable return. "You looked / as the lord looks down from a narrow window," she says to her husband, the first indication of the hierarchy in the family that will bear out in later poems, and he examines her, hand on his beard in a gesture that appears to signify analysis, objectivity of a kind that suggests emotional coldness for "the wife who runs out on the dock to write / as soon as one child is in bed." Clichés of artistic sacrifice notwithstanding, "Station" is the first appearance of a rare theme in Olds's poetry about another kind of loneliness in American life, the isolation of the writer, even from her own family. He looks down at her from the home, the family nest and her thematic center, surrounded by light in a tableau vivant that suggests two distinct spheres of relation and an implicit admission of neglect, even guilt on the part of the artist. The husband's reaction is notable in this regard: his "mouth, flexible as an archer's bow," barely moves despite the "long moment" the two spend regarding each other "in the truth" of their situation, "the poems / heavy as poached game hanging from my hands." A hunter like Diana, the poet is nevertheless a relatively powerless creation. This theme of marital complexity, as well as the husband as a figure outside his role as sexual partner, virtually vanish in Olds's poetry after "Station," only to be renewed as a driving dramatic force in her ninth book, *Stag's Leap,* which chronicles the couple's divorce.

In between these two extended statements, the husband appears sporadically across Olds's poems, often in celebrations of the sexual act or, in the overarching topos associated with his character, lionized by the poet. In "The Older" (68), from *The Unswept Room,* a poem about the aging of the female body, she admits, "I looked, to myself, / sometimes, like a crude drawing of a female . . . but this grayish, dented being is cozy as / a favorite piece of clothing, she is almost / lovable." But what appears to be a process of acceptance and personal growth turns in the poem on the gaze of the husband. "Of course," the daughter says, "it is / his love I am seeing, the working of his thumb / over" her body, which she describes as "this lucky nickel." In the next poem of the collection, "Fish Oil" (70), the poet dramatizes her wifely devotion by symbolically cleaning the domestic sphere (the husband has permeated the apartment with the funk of cooked fish and then gone to bed, leaving the mess to her) and reminds herself of his transformative power:

> I had come to my mate
> a shocked being, agog, a salt
> dab in his creel, girl in oil,
> his dish.

Much later in *The Unswept Room,* however, the poet admits to the eventual break in the relationship. "A Time of Passion" (109) develops like a typical paean to the sexual act ("Sex had been / like music, high and bright as the moon"), but then meaning in the poem turns, and the speaker refers to the empty nest in which "we were flying head / first into the earth and out," a typically surreal metaphor for the kinetics of dysfunction. Then in one of the overt statements that characterize her later writing, Olds says straightforwardly, "It never crossed my mind that he no longer / loved me, that we had left the realm of love." This admission is the first indication of the final plot point in the mostly submerged drama between the poet and her husband.

Stag's Leap

Stag's Leap (2012), Olds's Pulitzer Prize–winning ninth book of poems, is, like *The Father,* a single chronological narrative told in lyric vignettes. Its plot is driven by a love triangle: the poet's husband is leaving her for another woman. But the narrative takes into account only the actual relationship between husband and wife. Later this will include the poet's continued devotion to her mate as she attempts to recover from the breakup. Olds offers random clues about the character of the husband (he is a doctor and an artist) throughout the book, but like *The Father,* large sections of the story are left to be filled in by the careful reader, and the cast of characters—in this instance including the husband and his mistress, who is alluded to only as "the siren" in the title of a poem—are never directly described. If the reader is to construct them, they must do so from the speaker's reactions to them.

If one reads carefully, intimations of the failed marriage appear throughout the poetry, particularly in "Miscarriage" from *The Dead and the Living* (25), a powerful poem built on the raw details of the actual titular event. The poem is about the failures of nature and what they portend for the speaker and her husband. The fetus, barely a month old, appears like soil in "the pale / green swaying water of the toilet." Yet by the end of the poem, the speaker is made cognizant of its life force when she realizes that the "dark red like black" is actually "like forms of life / appearing" as sea life fungi. The sea is the cradle of all life, and fungi the most successful life-form on the planet. Humanity, even at the moment of biological failure, is conjoined with the kingdoms of life. When the poem turns to the poet's new child, rather than celebrating, she apostrophizes the husband with the recognition "that we could / botch something, you and I." The miscarriage becomes "a messenger / put to death for bearing bad news."

Stag's Leap begins at the moment the poet learns of her husband's infidelity and culminates in a brief meeting between the two in New York City. The book begins with a section that spans a year's time ("January–December") and then progresses to seasonally schematized sections ("Winter," "Spring," "Summer," and "Fall") that correspond to the poet's development through the ordeal. Finally the book leaps forward in its final section, "Years Later," when the couple meets in a city park, probably Central Park, several years before the 9/11 terrorist attacks. As with all Olds's collections, each section has its own themes, symbology, and narrative arcs. The title of the collection, and the logo on the cover of the original 2012 edition, comes from Stags' Leap, a winery outside of Napa, California. Wine is a vernacular symbol of love, and the poet references "a wine grown where I was born" in "The Flurry" (6). In the titular poem of the collection, "the label of our favorite red wine" evokes the husband "casting himself off a / cliff in his fervor to get free of me" (16). In a tradition that extends as far back as the Middle Ages, the stag is a heraldic symbol, often associated with sainthood or royalty, and a prey animal for the nobility. In Olds's loose allegory, her poetic speaker is a hunter and her husband a noble but elusive wild creature.

The overall narrative arc of *Stag's Leap* follows the downfall of the relationship. "January–December," the first section of the book, is composed of thirteen poems that ostensibly cover the final year of the couple's marriage. Many of the poems deal with the reasons why the marriage failed in paraphrased conversations. The first, "While He Told Me" (3), obliquely narrates the inciting incident: he has been unfaithful. Yet rather than displaying the expected anger, the poet wanders from room to room, "looked from small thing / to small thing." She actually flirts with the husband as he is in the shower and accepts his light touch on her face in bed before he rolls away and falls asleep. Olds's depictions of the familiarity and stilted affection hint at the reasons for their separation, and yet, avoiding the most obvious narrative traps, the story takes an unlikely turn. When they wake, the speaker cuddles him as he reads on the couch in their apartment—a homey, comfortable, familiar gesture on the morrow of such an admission. As is typical with Olds's poetry of the domestic sphere, she finds ironic symbolism for her situation in the small accoutrements of the household. In this case it is "two tulips stretched / away from each other" on a vase imprinted with an idyllic grotto scene that bares an "imagined shepherd in make-believe paradise."

"While He Told Me" initiates the humility topos that develops across the remainder of *Stag's Leap*. The narrator hints only sporadically about the rage that infidelity generally produces. "I show no anger but in flashes of humor," she says in "Unspeakable" (4), the second poem of the section. In this same narration, the husband refuses to discuss the mistress, thus marginalizing his wife even further. "I feel an invisibility / like a neutron in a cloud chamber," she responds, which can be juxtaposed to her own description of her married psyche: "When he loved me, I looked / out at the world as if from inside / a profound dwelling." The poem reverses the "it's not you it's me" cliché when the husband has the final word: "No, it's about / you, we do not speak of her." The poet in these lines accepts the implied guilt and subjugation of her own person. Any pride in self as subject, or in the feminine as a cultural object, is simply missing.

Likewise in the next poem in the sequence, "The Flurry," in which the couple discusses telling their children, the speaker expresses simply that "I feel I will love him / all my life." The expected rage boils to the surface only briefly when she imagines her tears as "a wirra of knives" thrown in a carnival act, "a heart's spurt / of rage." It is interesting to note that even in her most explicit expression, the action is only a performance. "I nod / to it" (the flurry of tears like knives), she says in the final lines, "it is my hope"; but the defensive aggression never materializes, and the weapons are never thrown. Instead she uses sympathetic and affectionate terms to describes her husband. Her one brief admission comes in a single rhetorical question buried in the titular poem:

> And when I wrote about him, did he
> feel he had to walk around
> carrying my books on his head like a stack of
> posture volumes.

Here the cheating husband is a martyr, restrained by the weight of his wife's poetry. In these moments the poet seems to take on the weight of the couple's failure, and once again her concern is for the husband's assumed feelings of exposure and inadequacy.

The next section, "Winter," dramatizes the natural longing that accompanies desertion. Again the expected rage is nowhere apparent, and the poet's self-analysis is predicated upon wifely failures. Poems such as "Not Going to Him" (25), which begins the sequence, evoke the melancholia of abandonment by tracing the physical traits of the husband's body. He is drawn with all his imperfections ("the knob that seemed to surface in his / wrist"; "the scar, doll-saucer of tarnish / set in time's throat"), almost as if the poet is ruminating upon a battered heirloom that traces her history. Physicality is, again, a central tenet of the poetry, the body a metaphorical map. And as with many of Olds's poems, recollection provides the primary action and description the primary tool. However revelation is not the same thing as clarification, and the poet's analysis often ends in self-deprecating confusion. She repeatedly implicates herself and her obsession with art for the failure of her marriage. For instance she implicitly justifies her husband's desertion in "Pain I Did Not" (SL 26) when she says,

> I think he had come in private, to
> feel he was dying, with me, and if
> he had what it took to rip his way out, with his
> teeth, then he could be born.

Birth is a significant metaphor given Olds's consistent use of motherhood in her poetry. In this case birth is violent and animalistic and signifies the failure of motherhood. In image and tone, the poet blames herself. She was naive about the realities of love and married life: she "had thought / a wedding promise was binding as a law / of physics" ("Approaching Godthåb," 39).

Despite such apparent clarity, she cannot completely parse her emotions. "My body may never learn / not to yearn," she says at the conclusion of "Not Going to Him"; conversely she wonders if yearning may be the "first farewell to him." Her question begins a never-completed process of healing. "They say now / that it does not work, unless you are equal," she says of marital love in "The Healers" (33), yet in the same poem she sees the husband and his mistress flying in tandem "like storks with the / doctor bags . . . dangling from their beaks" (the only intimation that the other woman is also a medical practitioner). This admission is both painful and telling: the poet conceives first of her own shortcomings (the balance of equality is weighted in favor of the husband) and then suggests that the new couple have achieved the equality lacking in her marriage. She take the fault for this on herself: "say there was / a god—of love . . . I had meant / to give—my life . . . I / had failed, well I could suffer for that" ("The Worst Thing," 27).

However, as the "Winter" section progresses, the poet comes to the conclusion that she misread the husband even as she idolized him. In "*Frontis Nulla Fides*" (28)—which roughly translated from Latin means "no reliance can be placed on appearance"—she recognizes that sometimes his eyes were "bleak or sullen" but that she conceived of them as "lakes" in which "one could sound them, and receive / no sense of their bounds or beds." As she did with her father, she has unconsciously deified the emotionally distant patriarch. He is linked with natural phenomenon that generally, in the vernacular symbols Olds tends to employ, stand for spiritual rejuvenation. At the same time, the poet recognizes that this was, in the terms of the poem, "illusion" and that "ignorant love gave me / a life." Later in the section, she limns the marriage as a shattered eggshell fallen out of the chimney ("On the Hearth of the Broken Home," 30) and then as a scenario in which the husband "went out by himself / into the boyhood place of deaths" while she, remaining in the domestic sphere, "lay in that bowl-of- / cream bed purring" ("Love," 31). In either case the poet implicitly convicts herself of self-delusion and, with self-depreciating irony, blames herself for sheltering in his home and taking him for granted.

"Spring," the next section, naturally follows and signifies rebirth. Yet the seasonal rebirth is qualified. In fact the symbolism is actually ironic. As "Winter" is set in a deadened world that lies fallow, so too the daughter's emotions should reawaken as life reawakens with the warming season. However, "Spring" in *Stag's Leap* does not fulfill this promise; rather its five poems provides a brief catalog of the haunting nature of loss.

"Once in a while, I gave up," the poet begins the initial poem of the section, "Once in a While I Gave Up" (43), "and let myself remember how much I'd liked the way my ex's / hips were set." She remembers, not surprisingly, the physicality of the husband, and she describes it with medical terminology and also with cosmic imagery reminiscent of her dying father. These details come "without / reserve, caution, or limit" from the "stubborn fundamentalist conviction" of the tactile sensations of her right hand. When Olds deals with erotic love, physicality and tactility are conduits to the amorphous, somewhat Platonic realm, implying that the body creates consciousness. In this regard she is a phenomenologist—a philosopher of physical experience—and the needs of the body equate to the needs of the heart.

Other poems in the section follow this basic theme of emotional distance contradicted by bodily desire: the husband is gone but not forgotten, creating a tidal pull of memories and recovery. Regret is embodied by a return to the couple's lost child in "To Our Miscarried One, Age Thirty Now" (44), also the subject of the earlier poem "Miscarriage." Here the poet acknowledges the limits of transitory emotion when compared with the permanence of mortality. This sentiment is immediately contradicted by "French Bra" (45), its companion poem, which acknowledges the power of memory and desire; triggered by the sight of chic French lingerie in a storefront window, the poet returns to the correlation between sexual union and emotional intimacy. For her the private rituals of the bedroom were "a club, with him, with secret / handshakes, and secret looks, and touches," and the accoutrements of this club constituted "our language." By the end of the poem, communion and the people who spoke to each other are only "the lingerie ghosts of my sojourn." Haunted by memory, she becomes a semiotician, literally reading the world through its signs and symbols. Love's hold on the mind, Olds suggests, is this profound.

Olds has created dichotomies throughout her work of dueling influences—in culture, in people's lives, in politics, and in mental health—and *Stag's Leap* narrows this focus down to a conflict between familial love and romantic abandonment and its lingering conflict in the psyche. "My Son's Father's Smile" (47) and "Not Quite Enough" (48) revive two familiar themes: paternal influence and the dangers of sexuality, respectively. In both poems the poet expresses her gratitude for her family and regret for limiting her husband's happiness. And each poem begins the same way, as she awakens from a dream, signaling her healing and emergence from illusion. But this renewal is tempered by guilt. The final image in the "Spring" section is from the poem "Not Quite Enough" (48): "I the glittering panther / holding him down, and screaming." Strength, a motif missing from the poet's self-portrait, finally manifests as a jungle cat—a type of exotic image rarely seen in Olds's poetry—yet her "scream" is ambiguous: is she screaming in rage, pain, or sorrow? Olds can be a mysterious poet, and meaning is often deliberately obscured. Considering the focus on the self in the confessional aesthetic, such moments indicate multiple meanings. The screaming panther represents the speaker's own ambivalence in the typical flux of lost love.

The poems in the next two sections, "Summer" and "Fall," blend together as a continuous series of elegiac meditations. Several imply linkage with the conjunction *and* or the conjunctive adverb *then* as the first word of the first line; this is an illusion of sequence, meant to imply that readers are involved in the poet's ongoing internal dialogue. This dialogue comprises recollections of typical domestic scenarios: a vacation home ("Sea-Level Elegy"); a failed lawn party ("Attempted Banquet"); a haircut while the husband is ill ("The Haircut"); and the discovery of candy bars hidden as gifts ("Discandied"). As is typical of Olds's artistry, these meager subjects become allegories and analogues. The beach cabin in "Sea-Level Elegy" (53) is a framework for remembrance—the poet finds reminders of her marriage on virtually every surface—that dramatizes the human inclination toward nostalgia. Nevertheless she concludes the poem with an admission either of strength or of weakness depending on how one reads the couplet: "I let myself go down where I have lived, and then, / hand over hand, I pull myself back up." "Attempted Banquet" (58), which concludes the "Summer" section, is a brief narrative about when the couple labored over a lavish backyard picnic only to be disappointing by the meager number of guests; the empty banquet is an allegory of the empty marriage overcompensated by the leftover food, a symbol of American indulgence, which lies like "carnage" beneath the "trees of life." In "The Haircut" (63), the poet cuts the husband's hair in order to "cheer him up" while he is sick; such devotion is an illusion, however, and the episode becomes a meditation upon death, symbolic of the delusion of living "forever with him." And "Discandied" (66) relates how the husband would hide candy bars around to house as surprise gifts when the poet was feeling blue. The verb *discandy* actually means to melt or dissolve (suggesting a clever play on words in the title), and its usage marks the turning point in the poet's attitude toward her marriage. After accidentally finding the hidden candy, she buries the chocolate in a compost pile "where the / potato sends its crisp shoots / of rage up." The potato is an odd choice of vehicle to describe rage—it is possible that Olds wants an image of faceless inertia springing into life—but then the poem recoils to a typically self-abasing realization. She recalls "how he hated it / when I tried to get him to talk to me . . . nagged him to reveal himself." Finally she concludes that "maybe these desserts were not only gifts, / but bribes or stops, to close my mouth." What briefly promises catharsis actually causes more humiliation and, upon inspection, the daughter's delusions of sympathy melt.

"Sleekit Cowrin'" (55) takes its title from the first line of Robert Burns's poem "To a Mouse," famous for its couplet "The best laid schemes o' Mice and Men / Gang aft agley." The overall theme of Burns's poem is the destructive power of human agency, symbolized by the plow that destroys the den of a mouse. In Olds's poem this conceit is an analogue to the destructive power of love. Other couplets from Burns's poem also reflect her sense of loss: "I'm truly sorry Man's dominion / Has broken Nature's social union," Burns's poem reads; "Thy wee bit housie, too, in ruin! / Its silly wa's the winds are strewin'!" Either of these couplets could be apt metaphors for Olds's speaker's own loss of home and comfort.

In the last poem of the "Fall" section, "Bruise Ghazal" (67), the polite fiction of the narrator character breaks, and the narrator reveals herself to be, in fact, Sharon Olds. The ghazal is a complicated poetic form of ancient Middle Eastern ancestry that also has a long lineage in English poetry. While Olds ignores the formal restrictions of the ghazal (which has to do with the number and composition of couplets), her poem follows the ancient rule that it should be about unrequited love. As such it is a fitting ending to the section dealing with the lost love. The poem's main conceit is "a black-and-blue oval on my hip," which is "sore as a lovebite, but too / large for a human mouth." For the first time, Olds acknowledges expression's limit through a neologism, *lovebite,* that links love and pain. Also for the first time Olds acknowledges that such spiritual damage is too large for a human mouth to speak or make.

Still this wound to the psyche heals over time, a function of life—as the body heals, so does the spirit. It is here, for the second time in the poetry (the first is "The Swimming Race" in *The Wellspring*), that the narrator identifies herself by name:

> Sleep now, Sharon,
> sleep. Even as we speak, the work is being
> done, within. You were born to heal.

Her injunction in the final line is to do no harm: "Since it cannot harm him, wound him, in your dreams." The dream image of the "glittering panther" from "Not Quite Enough" comes to mind, but in this instance sleep, death's second self, provides a safe zone where she attempts to build an ossuary for emotion.

If the collection had ended on this note, the elegiac disposition of *Stag's Leap* would take prominence, and the final message of the collection would be much different. But Olds continues the story. From here *Stag's Leap* skips forward to "Years Later," although, considering that the themes, style, and several of the settings (such as the beach and the couple's house) have already been established, this is a vague demarcation in the book. But the overarching theme of the "Years Later" section is the growth and reckoning of the narrator.

The first of the section's twelve poems is "On Reading a Newspaper for the First Time as an Adult" (71). The title is somewhat literal: the narrator castigates herself for not taking part in the world, symbolized by the newspaper, and by the end celebrates her new station as "a reader of the earth's gossip." The narrator characterizes reading the news as a distinctly masculine activity that she appropriates, refashioning the "paper-wasp nest" that the husband left lying around him in the morning like a shredded household. Yet what is a poem of self-congratulation and latent feminine empowerment turns in the final lines to a statement of mourning for the lost husband when she says,

> I weep to feel how I love to be like
> my guy. I taste what he tastes each morning
> without moving my lips.

In one sense "On Reading a Newspaper for the First Time as an Adult" is a poem about the power of the written word to reshape the individual. Through the act of reading, the reader takes on the power of the earth; she does not need to utter the words to "taste" the substance of life, all she needs is language to be empowered—a theme also found in the father poems. But again in the poetry, there is a limit to the power of language, and even as weeping is a sign of joy, it also represents sorrow. Still the theme of rejuvenation has been established, and the motion begun in the poem is carried forward through the "Years Later" section. By the third poem, "Slowly He Starts" (74), the daughter is able to acknowledge that "he is like / an icon, he is like a fantasy. / I did not know him, I knew my idea / of him." Similes and images of the husband in "Slowly He Starts" are of gigantic natural elements hovering literally in the sky over the planet like a "silver kite" that she cannot let go.

Poems from this point onward refine this theme until the final poem of *Stag's Leap* terminates in an ambiguous statement of acceptance. "Red Sea" (76), for instance, revisits the sexual implications of the biblical image first seen in "Animal Music" from *Blood Tin Straw,* but in this iteration, rather than a celebratory trope, the Red Sea is much closer to its original meaning as a passage over "dry / ground through the midst of the sea." In this iteration the narrator has finally found a passage out of bondage. The "waters / a wall unto me" are actually made of words, and "Red Sea" includes two columns of antonyms—some opposites through a sort of clever free association ("abandon, yoke, / desert surcingle")—representing again the dual nature of language both to constrain and to free the user.

The final five poems of *Stag's Leap* lead to the narrative's falling action. But it is debatable whether the conclusion merits a true denouement. In this final turn, the poet reiterates the notion that her husband's infidelity actually freed them both, reasserting (perhaps too vigorously) that their union was a mismatch. Yet in "Poem of Thanks" (82) she says,

> I want to turn to his departed back,
> and say, What gifts we had of each other!
> What pleasure—confiding, open-eyed,
> fainting with what we were allowed to stay up
> late doing.

Again the sexual act is a conduit to transcendent intimacy (and again a version of *le petite mort*) that is "allowed" by the sanctity of the marriage bed. In the next turn, however, the poet admits that the "touch you had from me" was for "*life,* like a sentence." What follows is a brief catalog of sexual exploits (on the beach by moonlight and once by daylight, in a barn, between the rows in a garden, up against the wall of a bathroom), for which she says, "thank you for every hour." While it begs the affective fallacy (in which the reaction on the reader is known), the question that tacitly pervades *Stag's Leap* concerns the expected reaction of the narrator: where is the rage of betrayal? Common experience would suggest that the jilted wife should react with melodrama. Part of what makes *Stag's Leap* such a unique statement about love and divorce—both common aspects of American life—is this focus on reconciliation and equanimity.

Such notions are qualified by the gender politics that undergird the story, but *Stag's Leap* seems to reject or at least nullify these politics in the interest of sustaining human interaction. Thus at the end of "Poem of Thanks," the narrator extends a (perhaps unnecessary) olive branch when she says, "let's part / equals, as we were in every bed, pure / equals of the earth." Again the link between sexual union and spiritual union is apparent, as is the symbol of life, the earth, knowledge of which the narrator gained through the reading of the newspaper.

A similar retreat from ire is found in "Left-Wife Bop" (83), a recollection about a bar of gold the husband retrieves from his old yard where he buried it years before, while he was still married to the narrator. Now cohabitating with his former mistress, the husband asks to return to the house he shared with his wife. The narrator's one request is that he not bring his girlfriend. Upon reflection she realizes the husband had returned for his buried treasure, presumably an asset that the couple shared. Predictably, however, the narrator says, "I didn't mind," and recalls how "even it was, between us, how even / we divided the chores." She wonders if her "bounty," symbolized by the buried gold, was a "kidnap fee." The husband perceives this, and like his unearthing the gold that he takes home to his girlfriend, he takes his love away from the earth that he shared with his wife. Also buried in the poem is the potentially deleterious effect of poetry itself; she reckons that "he did not give / his secrets to his patients, but I gave my secrets / to you, dear strangers, and his, too." This is the second time (the first is in "The Flurry") that the narrator acknowledges the effect of exposure, the panoptic nature of writing, on a real person. Her one hint of revenge—a sly subtheme in the collection—is the notion that poetic justice has been done. So, she concludes, "he was / redressing the balance, he was leading his own life." "Bop" refers to bebop, a style of jazz popular in the 1940s and 1950s, and Olds's title may be no more complicated than a sarcastic allusion to upbeat if sometimes discordant jazz; in this reading the poet is a scat singer and her husband her unwilling subject. But *bop* also denotes a light blow, particularly in juvenile slang, and this also seems to fit the scenario; the removal of gold from the ground that the couple once shared is a blow to the music of her poetry, albeit softened by memory.

The following two poems, "Years Later" (85) and "September 2001, New York City" (87), both deal with reunion. In "Years Later" the narrator acknowledges (perhaps conveniently) that the couple's affection was a lens for gender relations: men were mere "Ken dolls, all clothes," when she looked at them through her (now betrayed) married fidelity—now the former husband, she tells herself, is "married Ken." He is now only a man to her, one of the many she is no longer attracted to. Nonetheless, after he rejects her offer of further friendly meetings and dismisses her with "a dry bow," the narrator has a moment of romantic interfusion with the flora and fauna of the park ("green cemetery with no / dead in it") and reads an eminently romantic symbol of birdsong as a corollary to her own emotions. But rather than a living nightingale or thrush, the daughter spies "the body of a warbler," which looks to her "like a whole note fallen from the sky." She indeed equates the fallen bird to her "old / love for him, like a songbird's rib cage picked clean." Clearly the emotional wounds have not healed in the character.

"September 2001, New York City" (87) is, obliquely, an elegy for 9/11. In the opening lines, Olds acknowledges that "I said to a friend: I don't / think I could ever write about [the attacks]. / Maybe in a year I could write something." In this regard she mirrors the general expressive paralysis in the immediate aftermath of the attacks. It took time, as is generally the case, for writers to find their voices after a collective cultural trauma. Olds personifies one of the burning towers as a "huge, thrown, tilted jack / on fire," signifying the deadly game played by nations. But then the poem turns to an elegy for both her failed marriage and her mother. Removed from the context of *Stag's Leap,* "September 2001, New York City" is a poem of mourning and hope. The human condition is epitomized both by terrible destruction and by connection and solace as the narrator is "glad for [the husband] that he is with the one / he feels was meant for him." She is also heartened by her last moments with her mother; rather than traumatic separation, she remembers "the luck / and the luxury" of her last hour with her dying parent. Humanity will persevere, and those who do not die by violence must remember their luck.

The final poem of *Stag's Leap,* "What Left?" (89), reads like a summary of the major themes and conflicts in Olds's writing overall. Lines 1 through 10 deal with childbirth; lines 11 through 16 deal with the deaths of her mother and father; lines 16 through 29 deal with the reasons behind the failed marriage; and lines 30 through 32 culminate the poem and the collection with a unsurprising but still unlikely anaphora based on the notion that the couple "fulfilled something in each other":

> I did not deceive him, he did not deceive me,
> I did not leave him, he did not leave me,
> I freed him, he freed me.

Syntactic parallelism suggests equality between the two subjects, but the history of *Stag's Leap* contradicts this perception. As the final poem in the collection, "What Left?" seems to be a statement of denial, leaving readers to decide about the problematic theme of acceptance. The complete title could read "What Left *the Marriage*?" rather than, as might be expected, "*What's* Left of the Marriage?"

Stag's Leap appears to be an extremely personal message from a personal poet. Olds has bared herself and admitted to feelings that arguably contradict what an audience would expect. Olds has said of *Stag's Leap:*

> When I began reading the book, knowing its subject, I expected bitterness and anger. There was anger, but it surprised me that the book's main topic seemed to be love.
>
> To me, one of the important themes of the book is the difficulty some people have in being angry in self-defense. There are three or four poems in which I'm talking to myself about not idealizing. In the early poems in the book there's a lot of idealizing, which is really not love, as we know. It's not the love of the actual person, but kind of seeing that person as higher or better or more beautiful than he is.
>
> So for me, I like what you say, but for me it would be the interweaving of healthy anger and the recovery from idealization. Now it may not be angry enough to look like anger to anyone else, but there is a poem that says, "Since you cannot harm him, wound him." There's a kind of natural self-defense anger that this narrator doesn't seem to have at the beginning of the book—it seems more balanced at the end.[3]

As a final note, it is interesting to compare the portraits of the two principal patriarchs of the family narrative, the husband and the father. While Olds exploits the weaknesses of the father character, usually in anecdotal vignettes, the details of the husband are limited to expressionistic physical details, snippets of dialogue, and anecdotes that tend to ennoble him. The narrator is virtually always a victim of her father's alcoholic dysfunction, but in *Stag's Leap* she is the perpetrator of the husband's misfortune. The husband is acclaimed; the father is denigrated. The father fails at masculinity, weakening him, literally to death, leaving the narrator in a state of unresolved rage-cum-mourning; the husband embodies an austere manhood that carries him healthily out of the narrative frame, leaving Olds in a state of unexpressed anger-cum-mourning. The psychology behind this connection is ripe for deeper investigation.

CHAPTER 6

War, Suicide, Freaks

The Poet outside Herself

There are times when Olds steps away from the confessional mode to examine with humor and sympathy the world at large. In these instances she produces some of the best contemporary poetry. Each opening section of between nine and twelve poems in *The Dead and the Living, The Gold Cell,* and *One Secret Thing* contain lyrical progressions written from the point of view of a speaker who cannot be identified as any of Olds's usual characters. Instead these opening sections represent the more familiar limited-omniscient narrator who speaks subjectively about an experience, person, or people who she interprets, channeling the thoughts of her characters through her own voice or looking into their futures or their pasts. Poems in these opening sequences often take as their subject matter photographs of tragedies, victims of violence, historical personages, soldiers during wartime, the victims of war, and fictional narratives that illustrate the fragility of the human condition. And these poems consistently argue for clemency, mercy, and caring and against violence in all its forms. Olds's overarching theme in her poetry is to urge the reader toward empathy, and she is one of the few poets whose prime objective is the betterment of humanity. In this regard—in the overt nature of her purpose—Olds is something of a rarity in contemporary poetry. It is a generalization that holds true that poetry since the major theorists of modernism (T. H. Hulme, T. S. Eliot, and Ezra Pound) moved away from personal revelation. Poems should be "autonomous" in this philosophy, free of the constraints of the poet's personality, didactics, and formal structure, those features that (arguably) constrained the nature poets of previous generations. Between the great romantic and transcendental traditions of the nineteenth century and the literature that followed World War II, poetry focused on the artistry of language, image, and innovation. The confessional lyric passionately reinserted the personality of the poet and brought subjective emotional experience unmistakably back into the mix. In poems with the omniscient, outward-looking narrator—which can be thought of as her poems of the "nonconfessional" I—Olds's focus is on elegy and social justice. The following readings suggest the various approaches she takes to these poems. Olds's point in these examples seems to be cultural protest as opposed to the personal protest seen in her family poems. Her visions is broader, her arguments more overt, and her politics more exposed in these poems, many of which have their roots in the Cold War when they were written.

"When" (*TGC* 20), for instance, is a nuclear protest poem that, like virtually all protest poems about the atomic bomb, assumes the inherent evil of nuclear weaponry and the destruction of American civilization. Also typical of the protest genre, the poem likewise assumes a certain degree of innocence and helplessness on the part of the victims of nuclear Armageddon who can only stand as surprised, unwilling witnesses to their own demise. "When" was published in 1987, by which time American audiences were used to apocalyptic narratives about nuclear bombs and could readily imagine nuclear annihilation. In Olds's scenario war is a foregone conclusion: "I wonder now only when it will happen," the narrator says, and because she so often focuses on the plight of families, the scenario of the poem finds a young mother "holding her small daughter in her arms" as

> above the line of the trees,
> she will see rising, lifting up
> over our horizon, the upper rim of the
> gold ball, large as a giant
> planet starting to life up over ours.

Also because this is a narrative about an imagined war zone—an area that, because of the weaponry and geopolitical nature of this new combat, knows no geographical limits—the helpless civilians have no options except to watch. Then, with deliberate tragic irony, "the child will open her arms to it, / it will look so beautiful." "When" could be a companion piece to many antiwar poems that are easily as overt—Wilfred Owen's "Dulce et Decorum Est" or Thomas Hardy's "The Man He Killed." What is unique about Olds's concept is the tameness of the situation. Pop-culture Armageddon is generally sensational: crowds panic in the streets; cities disintegrate under blinding detonation; the landscape is rendered an irradiated wasteland. But Olds gives readers an almost sentimentalized vision of the event. A child opens her arms to the rising fireball because, in her blamelessness, she finds it pretty. The argument is implicit but clear—won't somebody please save the children? If there is a weakness to the poem, it is this clarity of purpose that borders on overstatement. If nothing else, "When" reflects a conundrum of poetry—is a lyric a failure when its meaning is so overt?

A more reserved antiwar poem is "Japanese-American Farmhouse, California, 1942" (*TW* 6). This short lyric is imagistic, allowing the deserted house, which no longer contains a family, to dramatize quietly the internment of Japanese Americans during World War II. "I was born, that day, near there, / in wartime, of ignorant people," Olds has written, implicating her parents but also a generation of white Americans who imprisoned their fellow citizens because of paranoia and racism. The quietude of the poem resonates with the silence of generations after World War II, both Japanese American and white, who justified, denied, or ignored this outrage. All Olds's war poems are statements for peace, and human beings always provide the pathos in her arguments. The narrator admits her nearness to bigotry (she was born in 1942 in San Francisco) as she indicts her own heritage.

Similarly political to a fault, "Republican Living Rooms" (*SS* 16) is a poem that is so overt and hyperbolic that its imprecations against patriarchy and gendered violence reduce it to agitprop. Largely a tableau, the poem begins with allusion to T. S. Eliot's "Love Song of J. Alfred Prufrock": "I have known the Republican living rooms," the speaker says, evoking modernist disaffection with a culture of "oversize furniture," "overstuffed linen," "coffee-tables heavy as map-tables / in some war room," and "table-lamps large and brutal." She speaks here of brutish conspicuous consumption and the heavy accoutrements of jingoistic masculinity. The final victim in all this is a woman pinned to the floor of the drawing room by the host of the party, "her face streaked with blood." Her death gives pleasure and purpose to the Republican host, and "best of all, it costs / absolutely nothing." This is an example of Olds's politics made overt and, again, arguably bathetic in its attempt to portray domestic violence.

"Electricity Saviour" from *Blood Tin Straw* (112) is a more restrained example of a mysterious speaker, apparently unassociated with the arc of the collection, who tells the story of a young man, perhaps the male child character, sneaking through the house and turning off stray lights while on an apparently self-appointed, ecoconsious mission to save energy. "Electricity Saviour" revolves around a series of narrative snippets in which a young man of indeterminate age "patrols the house" for excess lights and turns them off. The family lives "in partial dusk, / banging our shins" as the boy turns off bulbs and chandeliers because "he knows and believes / that a continent could die."

At the same time, the poem suggests a typical critique of the family dynamic: the boy spies around doorjambs to find "his father in a wasteful pool" of light, "his mother in another, his sister shut / in her room with her hoarding of power." Once again the modern world, particularly modern America and its consumptive personality, segments the essential family unit into alienated components, each in their own pool of personal expenditure. Greed, always a perceived sin in American culture, has segmented the nuclear family. The boy stands against this consumptive, disruptive worldview. The rest of the family "seems willing to use the world up." Here the boy metaphorically saves the planet; precious, even numinous, he clutches the earth to himself "like a lamp." In similar instances Olds uses light as a motif for life, particularly family life (see the discussion of *The Father*), and in the instance of "Electricity Saviour," light represents both the health of the family, as if it is a single organic entity, and the health of the culture, for which the family is a cellular member. Contextually, however, the poem may be about the differences between generations, symbolized by the ecological concerns of the youth juxtaposed to the consumerism of his parents.

The Dead and the Living: "Poems for the Dead"

The first section in *The Dead and the Living,* "Poems for the Dead," stands as a perfect example of Olds's outward-looking poetry. Comprising nine lyrics, "Poems for the Dead" is based upon pictorial representations of human brutality and environmental tragedy. The section moves chronologically across the globe, beginning in China in 1905, moving through race riots in Tulsa and the Iranian Cultural Revolution, and into the present moment of Chilean dictatorship. As a whole "Poems for the Dead" represents the communal dangers of both humanity and nature, and Olds's purpose, as always, is to argue for empathy.

"Poems for the Dead" is divided into two sections with deceptively simple titles: "Public" and "Private." The "Public" section concerns what it means to be part of a community, with what one does pertaining to or affecting that community. The word can also refer to being in service to a community or acting on its behalf. It can also mean being under a community's control. All of these definitions apply to the first section, which at first glance seems embroiled in the inhumane aspects of community.

"Ideographs" (5) is as disturbing as can be expected for a poem that initiates such a sequence, yet the poem carries the implicit charge to the reader to fight first-world complacency and be actively engaged in amnesty. An ideograph is a symbol or picture that stands in the place of a word; in the West the term is used generally associated with the languages of Asia. For this reason

Olds's choice of title—which might at first seem politically incorrect or inappropriate given the subject matter of crucifixion—carries the important weight of the poem: words, "ideographs," represent people. People are what say and do for their community, and they are also what determines community control.

As with the other titles of the section's poems, "Ideographs" is deceptively simple in construction and purpose: it describes a picture taken, as the epigraph explains, in China in 1905. A number of photographs taken by Western journalists and Western soldiers stationed in China in the late nineteenth and early twentieth centuries sensationalized Chinese corporal punishment for European audiences of the time. These images—which include beheading, punishment by constriction, public shaming, and the infamous *Ling Chi,* which has come down through popular culture as "Death by a Thousand Cuts"—helped fuel Eurocentric perceptions of Asian primitivism and European cultural superiority. Nevertheless images of Chinese corporal punishment are disturbing representations of cruelty. By speaking through the voice of the victim, Olds implores readers to take action for the victims of all tragedy, human-caused and otherwise, a sentiment that resonates through the rest of the poems in the book and through Olds's entire oeuvre.

"Ideographs" describes two men (presumably criminals, although what crimes have been committed, political or otherwise, are unknown) crucified upon "small scaffolds, boards in the form of / ideographs"—in the form of words, that is, with their important implications for readers and humanity in general. Significantly one scaffold "is the simple / shape of a man," signaling the link between the torture device and the man it carries; he is, in other words, the artifact that support him. If people's words, as with their devices, are brutal, so are they. The photograph has captured the last moments of the prisoners' lives and, most important, the brutality of their sentences before they are to be carried ritualistically through the screaming crowd. "Ideographs" is most likely based upon a series of readily available photographs. Much of its power comes from its pictorial nature. The poem is largely reportage, as the speaker describes the bent limbs, the wrists nailed to the boards, the face of the man looking directly into the camera. Such blunt depiction in verse transfers the raw power of the picture into words. Olds focuses on the painful and grotesque realities of torture, even as the narrator remains calm and objective almost to the point of disinterest:

> The man on it
> is asleep, his arms nailed to the wood.
> No timber is wasted; his fingertips

> curl at the very end of the plank
> as a child's hands open in sleep.

Yet this forensic precision, these minute details carefully selected, is what sums the horror of the situation, made all the more disturbing by the image of a child's hand in sleep. But it is the other man, the one who is awake, that carries the significance of the scene—"He looks at us in the silence," the narrator relates. "He says / '*Save me, there is still time.*" Act now, Olds urges, before it is too late.

The next three poems in the section—"Photograph of the Girl," "Race Riot, Tulsa, 1921," and "Portrait of a Child"—are all based on specific photographs taken during tragedies in 1921. The images come from Russia, Oklahoma, and Armenia, respectively. Each poem investigates a singular human tragedy—drought, racism, and genocide—and so depicts natural disaster, American racial politics, and ethnic cleansing, all age-old forces that humanity must contend with in the cycles of survival and civilization. "Photograph of the Girl" (6) could be any of a number of photographs taken during the dreadful Povolzhye famine. Again Olds focuses on close details of the victim; she is "stunned, / eyes closed, mouth open, / raw hot wind blowing / sand in her face." Such scrutiny asks readers to empathize with the victim, a sensation that Olds magnifies by focusing on her adolescence, which will never come to fruition. The caption to the picture indicates that she will "starve to death that winter / with millions of others." Yet the greatest tragedies are the generations that are never to be born, signified when the girl's "ovaries let out her first eggs, / golden as drops of grain."

Olds then turns to one of the worst racial confrontations in American history in "Race Riot, Tulsa, 1921" (7). As with the preceding poems, "Race Riot" is based on a photograph taken during the event itself. It describes an almost pedestrian scene taken after the turmoil is over. There is little actual dynamism in the photograph—the people march subdued and calmly into the courthouse, overseen by white armed guards. In this world, however, "the blazing white shirts of the white men / are blanks on the page" so bright that "looking at them is like / looking at the sun, you could go blind." Juxtaposed to this overwhelming and dangerous whiteness with its machine guns and racial hatred, "the dark glowing skin of the women and / men going to jail" provide visual and moral counterpoint. The poet's gaze then descends to the real focus of the poem, the body of a black man lying on a flatbed truck, "shoes pointed North and South" to symbolize the divisions in the American racial landscape. The speaker reads the man's corpse as if he is an ideogram of sorts, "his face tilted up / toward the sky, to get the sun on it, to / darken it more and more toward the color of the human." It is an odd moment in what is clearly a protest poem aimed at the long history of racial violence in the United States. Again the animating principle is empathy for the victim of communal violence and, in the background, the notion of social justice.

The third 1921 poem, "Portrait of a Child" (8), once again implies that the truest tragedy of the starving child is the effect on the unborn. This poem is based upon a disturbing picture taken in Yerevan, a city established by Armenians who survived the Turkish genocide of 1915 until the 1920s, as indicated by the epigraph to the poem. The power of "Portrait of a Child" lies in its descriptiveness, in the simple depiction of starvation.

> His face is quite peaceful, really,
> like any child asleep, though the skin
> is darkened in places, the curved eyelids
> turgid, part of the ear missing
> as if bitten off.

In such moments Olds uses a maternal perspective—signified by a series of motifs privileging images and metaphors of children as if described by a motherly speaker. As always she turns to sex: a dead child's penis lies "pale and lovely there," desexualized, but ever the reminder of "the children he would have had."

The fifth of the "Public" poems, "Nevsky Prospekt" (9), is placed out of chronology (the epigraph reads "July 1917") but is a logical conclusion to the photo-based poems within the section. The Nevsky Prospekt is a large street in Saint Petersburg, Russia, also the site of a clash between soldiers of the Russian Provisional Government (established after the abdication of Czar Nicholas II) and protestors angered by years of shortages and unemployment. The photograph, taken from a high angle on a rooftop, immortalizes civilians running from a blast of automatic gunfire. It is "an old photo, very black and / very white," which is literal (as it describes the composition accurately) and polemical (as it suggests there is an absolute wrong captured in the aged celluloid). Political and historical perspectives are elided in the actual texts of these poems—as is the case in other poems that utilize the radium girls, woman cannery workers, or abandoned babies—to focus on the people involved. This technique is eminently viable in the information era, forcing the interested reader to seek the facts, almost as one is forced to read a poem closely to understand its meaning. It is debatable whether or not such searching adds to the presentation of these poems, however. The fact that the July 1917 clash immortalized in picture and poem was a part of the Russian Revolution adds depth to the image, but this knowledge also deflects from the violence done by and to humanity. Protest poetry is a quiet, intellectual vehicle. But this is not Olds's style. She is much more interested in a broad empathetic challenge than a narrow political one. And she wants to be brash, loud, even offensive to get readers' attention. Thus "Nevsky Prospekt," like her other political-cum-personal poems, distills conflict down to individuals, victims and perpetrators, the human stories behind the image. Against the individual is the mechanism, literal and metaphoric, of war; "Nevsky Prospekt" ends on the notion that violence will destroy the power of the individual to speak through "the terrible / voice of the submachine guns saying / *This is more important than your life.*" For Olds, an American author writing during the Vietnam War, the fact that the Russian riot took place on July 4 adds another layer of irony.

Amid these poems of famine and war, Olds abruptly, without apparent contextualizing, turns to a tragedy of American popular culture. In 1962 Marilyn Monroe died of barbiturate overdose, possibly suicide, at the age of thirty-six. Olds focuses not on the star's untimely death but on the effect her passing has on the paramedics who handled her corpse. "The Death of Marilyn Monroe" (10) revolves around a single dramatic premise: "These men were never the same." Olds's poem alleges that "their lives took / a turn" into "nightmares strange / pains, impotence, depression." In this new world, "his [the paramedic's] wife looked / different, his kids. Even death" had changed. The other paramedic "found himself standing at night . . . listening to a / woman breathing, just an ordinary / woman / breathing." Monroe was incomparable, the poem implies, and her death signaled the death of an ideal. Ordinary women cannot compare now that the icon of public sexuality has been removed, and Olds again reasserts the power of the male gaze not only to influence men but also to change the concept of womanhood.

The placement of "The Death of Marilyn Monroe" among poems that deal with tragedy on a large scale brings into focus a number of themes—the dangerous lives of women, even iconic women, in the Western world, which is so often removed from the large-scale horrors of nature and genocide; the American obsessions with fame and conspiracy; the worship of the female body; the sensationalization of death; and America's own myopic interest in its celebrities—yet it is a tragedy nevertheless. Her death brings the previous poems, and the following poems—on the Shah of Iran and "Things That Are Worse than Death" (13), about violence and oppression—into the private realm, not coincidently the title of the next section in *The Dead and the Living.* But it is the concluding couplet of "The Issues" (11), a poem about Rhodesia, that might sum up Olds's philosophy overall: "Don't speak to me about / politics. I've got eyes, man."

The Gold Cell: Part 1

"Summer Solstice, New York City" (3), which initiates the opening sequence of *The Gold Cell,* is a strangely compassionate and uplifting poem considering that its subject is an attempted suicide. This ultimate violence upon the self, rather than fracturing social or moral bonds, actually fashions a natural, primordial connection between people. Or to be more precise, how people react to violence upon the self illustrates the native compassion of the species and changes the environment, suggesting how civilization is built from communal care. Whereas her intimate personal portraits tend toward the humiliating and dysfunctional, Olds's broader poems about humanity in peril or pain reveal a deep empathy. As a prime example of this theme, "Summer Solstice, New York" is a narrative poem about the ability of human beings, particularly the dominant power structure, to provide solace. This vision offers a rare counterpoint to Olds's other political poems, which deal with power structures, and suggests that the base of power is community and its healing potential.

Olds's bedlamite in "Summer Solstice, New York" climbs to a city rooftop on "the longest day of the year" when, presumably, the pain of living has found its greatest duration. The earth is used in several instances as a symbol for humanity's sharing space as a kind of communion ("Left-Wife Bop" [*SL* 83], "A Time of Passion" [*TUR* 109], and "Earth Aria" [*TUR* 71]), and in this instance the northern hemisphere of the Earth is tilted so that it is at its closest proximity to the sun, the source of light and life on the planet. In the pagan tradition, the summer solstice symbolizes the power of light over darkness. The Latin root word, *solstitium,* translates as "the sun stands still." From this point in the planet's calendar, the days (signifying life) begin to get shorter, while the nights (signifying death) begin to get longer. Farmers are done with their planting by this time of the year, and the warm season of growing has reached its zenith, with the weather sliding toward the cold winter season. In the Roman tradition, the summer solstice was a holiday dedicated to Juno, the queen of the gods, and her relationship to childbirth. Olds is careful about her titles—they are always meant as a guide to reading the poem—and one should not overlook the importance of these traditions, particularly the implications of light versus dark and day versus night, in the interpretation of the poem. Despite the scenario death is a moment of celebration, even renewal.

In "Summer Solstice, New York City," when the young man puts "one leg over the complex green tin cornice," marking the edge of his life, he has actually made the first overture, the first cry for help, to his fellow humans; he pauses and warns that "if they came a step closer that was it." Here, in moments such as these, Olds demonstrates her prowess as a poet. It would be easy to sentimentalize and overdramatize such an intense scenario, particularly when a theatrical imperative has been established at the outset. One is reminded of Hart Crane's "bedlamite" leaping from the Brooklyn Bridge with his "shrill shirt ballooning" around him in *The Bridge*. Olds resists the impulse to become expressionistic and opts for an essentially minimalistic diction in the poem. And with abruptness of minimalism, the narration turns, despite the overtones of celestial nature, to the corporate, automatic, automated response of sympathy. "The huge machinery of the earth began to work for his life," the poem reads, actually describing the human agency that intercedes in the most severe form of violence, the violence against the self and all its emotional dislocation. Again, however, "earth" is a symbol of communion even as the poem presents a particularly unromanticized vision by taking in the practical, bureaucratic nature of law enforcement: "one put on a bullet-proof vest," the narrative reads, "a black shell around his own life, / life of his children's father." As always Olds lauds the responsible parent, taking note of the importance of family on the moral character of the actor. What seems for the moment a call to corporatized violence is actually an expression of paradoxical tenderness, a moment the narration compares to motherhood, Olds's default for human kindness:

> And they closed on him, I thought they were going to
> beat him up, as a mother whose child has been
> lost will scream at the child when it's found, they
> took him by the arms and held him up and
> leaned him against the wall of the chimney.

When the police captain lights a cigarette, he hands it to the young man, and the narrative is allowed to achieve its expected, even needed, emotional height. The "red, glowing ends" of the cigarettes remind the narrator of "tiny campfires we lit at night / back at the beginning of the world." This is a perfect example of Olds's vernacular symbolism: the campfire is, as is so often the case with the public symbols in Olds's poetry, an almost too familiar reminder of childhood, summer vacations, and the friendly side of nature. Fire here is warm and comforting. Yet Olds here has gone even further to suggest the tribal beginnings of civilizations when humanity was primarily small family clans fighting for survival in a wild world. The simple act of sharing a smoke, yet another vernacular symbol (this time from popular culture), signifies the job is over and well done. The "gold hole they say is in the top of the head" may refer to the seventh chakra in the Hindu religion, representing wisdom and enlightenment and located at the crown of the head. This, the poem suggests, is how people should react to each other.

The three poems that follow "Summer Solstice, New York"—"On the Subway," "The Abandoned Newborn," and "In the Cell"—offer opposite visions of humanity, however. "On the Subway" (5), the second poem of part 1, is also a city poem, a tableau poem, and a meditation upon white privilege. While riding the subway, the narrator, who identifies herself as Caucasian, sees a young African American man with the "casual cold look of a mugger, / alert under hooded lids," sitting opposite her. His choice of clothing outwardly exposes the internalized wounds of history and culture: he wears "black sneakers / laced with white in a complex pattern like a / set of international scars" and "red, like the inside of the body / exposed." She, on the other hand, wears "dark fur, the / whole skin of an animal." It is an honest admission that her life is remarkably different from his. He bears the white history on his feet (as if still in the shackles of slavery), while his body is outfitted in red, the natural color of violence, even war, and the rendered body, and a significant color during an era when youth violence was often associated with African American teens; the young man is, in short, clothed in the uniform of a member of the Bloods gang. Ultimately, though, the narrator comes to the unfortunate realization that, while she means no harm, "I must profit from his darkness," meaning that she accidentally profits from his racial history despite herself, as he must suffer from the whiteness that foments racial divide and street violence. In some respects the poem plays it safe. Olds's analysis comes to the expected politically correct conclusion, yet it is a brave statement nevertheless, and an unusual one for twentieth-century poetry written by a white person. Olds openly tackles the dangerous topic of race relations without the palliative assurance that, if we just look beyond the skin, we can all get along. Olds refuses simple, reductive, and appealing platitudes for the harder but arguably more truthful position that culture shapes and perhaps confines the individual. If "Summer Solstice, New York" is about the natural tendency of the species for compassion, then "On the Subway" is a poem about the scars of history.

The third poem of the first section in *The Gold Cell* takes the unfortunately common scenario of child abandonment in "The Abandoned Newborn" (7). Somewhere between sixty and a hundred newborns are abandoned each year in the United States, although there are no authoritative studies on the exact number. Many of these do not survive their abandonment. The newborn in the poem, who is wrapped only in a plastic supermarket bag, represents the sundering of the natural order by some destabilizing force (perhaps capitalism) in American culture. The poem is indefinite in this regard. Nevertheless Olds identifies this child as "the most American baby, / child of all of us through your very / American parents." Of course this is not a strictly American problem, and it would be unfair to suggest that only Americans are capable of this sort of behavior, but Olds's purpose is a condemnation of America's culture of disposable products. Again the notion of the family as central to the well-being of society undergirds the poem, and Olds welcomes the abandoned child into society, almost as if the poem is a benediction for a survivor.

In the fourth poem of the section, "In the Cell" (9), Olds again ruminates upon man's inhumanity to man. In this case it is men, specifically, that she is writing about. "In the Cell" is a poem about the incomprehensibility of torture, yet it explains torture as a product of power, an apparently masculine syndrome that destroys the natural potential for man to procreate and provide. The scenario begins innocently (and safely) enough as the narrator rides in the front seat of the family car and notices the hairs on her legs in the sunlight. Her body hair is thinning with middle age, she notes to herself, part of the natural progression of family. This is a wholesome moment, as the sunlight illuminates the front seat and the children laugh in the back, familiar to American middle-class families. Yet with the sort of free association typical to private thought, the narrator wonders at those others, the faceless men in an unnamed war scenario, who mutilate their prisoners to extract information. The narrator muses specifically about the "youth," as opposed to her stolid adulthood, who tortures another young man in order to extract information about people, places, and things that the torturer can then conquer. She is specific about the torturer's technique of "taking a man's genitals off as / slowly as possible." What at first might seem simply a gratuitous reference thrown in for shock value is actually symbolic of extinguished unborn generations. Within Olds's private symbology, sex, genitals, and sexual union are not treated with embarrassment but emphasized for their biological, and thus spiritual and historical (for the sake of the species), significance. The destruction of the body in this case is the destruction of culture. To make the connection between conquest and culture clear, the torturer needs language from his victim—literally names and maps in "our common tongue and / written with our usual alphabet"—in order to, in the narrator's words,

> rule those maps, change the names of the streets and
> line the people along them to turn the
> small cells of their faces up to him,
> the sun on him like gilding.

This line is a perversion of the "common tongue," a brutality linked to the conqueror's delusion that the sun will then "gild" him like a statue or a god. The sanctity of family, the authority of language, the sexual organs as the reservoir of future generations, the implicit argument for kindness and an end to violence, all these familiar themes are encompassed in "In the Cell." As a movement within the sequence of poems, the poet quickly, adroitly traverses the modes of primal human life, from desperation and community to pathology and compassion, to the brutal lust for power, all aspects of the human condition that Olds investigates with unflinching attention. At the same time, there is a certain superficiality to the meditation and a lack of awareness of the forces that shape the torturer and the tortured. This shallowness could either be a strength (of verisimilitude: few Americans have had firsthand experience with the subject of this poem) or a weakness (of pretention: an overly simplistic vision of violent political turmoil).

"The Twin" (10), on the other hand, offers an unlikely vision of connection. The poem is dedicated to a Lazarus Batista Colloredo. Colloredo had a "brother," Joannes, who grew out of his chest cavity as a case of parasitic twinning. Joannes (named after John the Baptist) seems never to have gained consciousness. If touched he exhibited what appeared to be basic motor reactions—his lips and eyes would move, for example—but he showed no sign of real consciousness. The conjoined brothers toured Europe in the mid-seventeenth century, visiting Turkey, Germany, and France, among other countries, even visiting the royal court of Charles I of England. When not on display, Lazarus covered his sleeping brother with a cloak so as not to attract undue attention. Contemporary accounts of Lazarus report that he was courteous and well-spoken, and he was reputed to have eventually sired a number of physiologically normal children.

This story forms the basis of Olds's meditation upon the strangeness of biology and the triumph of humanity. It is a tender poem. While much of its thrust is dedicated to examining the freakishness of the conjoined bodies—particularly the strangeness of the unconscious twin, who Olds refers to with the gender-neutral pronoun *it* and limns via his most inhuman characteristics ("its arms—jointed like / chicken wings—springing from its ribs and / held with slings")—there is an undeniable note of empathy for the unfulfilled pseudo life of the twin. Her diction is typically vernacular and minimalist, the portrayal matter-of-fact, and yet the close attention to the twin's face highlights his basic humanity:

> Its eyes are closed
> and never did open. Its mouth is open
> and never did close, and though along the jaws
> whiskers appeared, from the mouth there never
> came a sound.

Joannes's genitals are "buried" in his conscious brother's body, symbolizing the impossibility of his lifeline and the possibility his presence will continue through his progeny. But the poem turns on the fact that Lazarus "had it [Joannes] baptized, naming the heart next to his heart." Olds here takes note of the fact that Joannes was not named at birth (even if the poem does not explain this) and that, probably expressing a brotherly tenderness for the pseudo man whose nonlife hemmed in his own life, Lazarus has his twin named and baptized. What Olds brings into focus is the redemptive power of humanity. In redeeming his brother, the unconscious twin takes on the messianic role of the biblical Baptist, and the living Lazarus is led through the world by "the one he named John the Baptist, who goes before him into the wilderness." Through the act of faith, an aberration of nature has achieved a connection to the human and to the divine, and both brothers are saved.

Another poem from the same section, "The Girl" (14), is one of Olds's most brutal. "The Girl" is an unflinching poem of sexual violence and a polemical portrait of survivors and perpetrators. Focused on the dehumanizing act of male sexual aggression, it is stark, almost journalistic, in its approach to the crime of rape. "They chased her and her friend through the woods / and caught them in a small clearing," the first lines read. The abruptness and vagueness appear deliberate here, with the chase ending in a setting created by the fallen world of disposable America:

> broken
> random bracken, a couple of old mattresses,
> the dry ochre of foam rubber,
> as if the place had been prepared.

"The Girl," as is the case with poems such as "The Abandoned Newborn," is set in a culture that destroys and pollutes itself. Olds's description of the actual attack is minimal and nonmetaphoric. She describes, again with journalistic reserve, the stabbing, cutting, and shooting of the victims, and the chilling words of the young man ("*Now you're going to know what it's like / to be shot 5 times and slaughtered like a pig*") are delivered without editorial contextualizing. Details about the rapists are sparse: one is "thin with black hair," and the other is simply "the blond one." Likewise the victims are rendered only as "two naked 12-year-old girls." Objectivity, narrative distance, terseness of style, and minimal descriptions are meant to both intensify the shock value—readers are left with the facts of the matter, just as they would be in a news report, and suddenly the coldness with which terrible crimes come to public attention is manifested in poetry, one of the most intimate of art forms. Additionally the generic nature of the rapists and victims suggests that the story could have occurred anywhere in the United States.

The focalizing lens of "The Girl" then switches from a distant omniscient narrator to the perspective of one of the girls. As she loses consciousness, scenes of home and motherhood flash and then fade out before her eyes. These images—of the "globes of light on the rounded / lips of her mother's nesting bowls" in the kitchen at home—are carefully chosen to represent the softness ("rounded"), humanity ("lips"), and comfort ("nesting") of the domestic sphere. The girl survives and wakes to find a mattress "pulled over her" to hide her body, yet it is "like a / blanket at night." The soiled mattress is a perversion of the comfort and sanctity of the bed, symbolic sites of family and procreation. Deliverance is still the provenance of the world of men, however: as she steps naked from the forest, the symbol of the wilderness of human violence, she encounters a railway brakeman and pleads, "*Please, sir. Please, sir.*"

From the outside it appears that the girl returns to her community and is, at least provisionally, accepted, celebrated even. But Olds's meaning is anything but comforting. Sorcha Gunne and Zoë Brigley Thompson offer an excellent reading of the poem:

> Although the girl does rebuild her life, she is always a site of uneasiness for the rest of the community. Even when she adopts the conventional roles of cheerleader, student and daughter, the town cannot see past the crime. As a symbol of sexual violence, she is an inconvenient and disturbing reminder of the dark side of human experience—all the more so because the rape is not a bizarre crime committed by outsiders, but an act performed by the brothers and sons of the town. Olds concludes that the girl has found out "what all of us never want to know" and so cannot be accepted back into the community.[1]

Often considered a crime that implicates the victim, rape tends to become an indelible and defining mark affecting how the survivor is seen and understood socially. The girl prays for her dead best friend every night and "then thanks God for life" and as a cheerleader performs sexualized splits and cartwheels, but the final image is one of sublimated rage and psychological mutilation: "she shakes the / shredded pom-poms in her fists."

The final poem in the "Private" section of *The Dead and the Living*, "Absent One," (28), is dedicated to Muriel Rukeyser. The elegy limns a few sparse details of the subject's illness ("how white you are, how thin you are") that blossoms metaphorically into "a flowering / branch suspended over my life." What begins in mourning transforms into a lyric of love and victory. Among the repeated visions of family disharmony, male violence, and hegemonic patriarchy, Olds provides a brief, mournful, celebratory lyric of poetry's sisterhood.

One Secret Thing: "War"

Part 1 of *One Secret Thing* (2008) is simply titled "War." This collection was published five years into Operation Iraqi Freedom and a year after the "New Way Forward" surge increased the number of U.S. troops in Iraq to more than 182,000. At the same time, the Pentagon estimated that more than 100,000 civilians had fallen victim to terrorist bombings in the region since 2003. While Olds does not specifically reference the occupation of Afghanistan and Iraq in the "War" section, it seems apparent that this conflict provides the backdrop for a series much like "Ideograms" in which descriptions of photographs form an implicit protest. These short, imagistic poems focus on civilians, sometimes far away from the actual battles, as victims of violence and on soldiers (who are all men) as victims of their own militarism. As is always the case, Olds's overarching implicit call to action is to end violence, for the sake of both victims and perpetrators.

Properly speaking, "War" is a single, numbered sequence of twelve discursive lyrics, tableaus, and vignettes. The first poem is "Woman with the Lettuce" (7). As in "Ideographs," Olds opens with a character looking directly at the reader as if into a camera lens. Much of the brief tableau is spent describing "an oversized lettuce, its white stems and / great, pale, veined leaves / unfolded in the dense air." The lettuce represents life—as does every article owned by people in the section—threatened by warfare. Still the emphasis is on the woman as she is shoved toward a truck; the scene could be virtually any place, any war, in which civilians are collateral damage.

In "Legless Fighter Pilot" (8), Olds describes the contortions that the legless pilot must perform in order to climb into his airplane: "right calf in his hand, / [he] lifts the whole leg up, straight," as if his severed limb is simply an implement; likewise the "left leg he / bends by hand at the knee, pulls it in, and / slams the hatch." In the sky, however, human limitations do not matter. The scene most likely describes the World War II fighter ace Douglas Bader, a pilot who lost both his legs in an airplane crash in 1930 and quit flying for the RAF; Bader had scarcely been flying two years at that time.[2] Despite his handicap he was recommissioned at the beginning of World War II, scored numerous kills, and was promoted. As a squadron leader, his tactics were successful but considered hazardous, and Bader was repeatedly forced to answer to his superior officers. He is credited with numerous kills, strategic brilliance, and extraordinary skill as a pilot, but he lost as much as 50 percent of those under his command. Bader represents the brave and capable warrior who wounds himself while wounding his enemy; the society of violence hurts the violent too. As with her other historical protest poems, this background is largely absent, perhaps even unnecessary, and forces the interested reader to interpret facts outside the frame of the poem.

The next three poems all deal with the pointlessness and indignity of warfare. In "What Could Happen" (9), partisans are murdered by a band of soldiers simply designated as "the others." These nameless, faceless soldiers will cut their "sexual organs . . . to destroy the mold" of humanity, and yet the partisans are given symbolic rebirth when new comrades spring up as if "from the loam dark as the body's wound." The poem has a synonymous theme with Carolyn Forché's antiwar poem "The Colonel." In Leningrad in 1914, according to "The Dead" (10), winter was so cold that coffins became firewood. The dead "lay on the snow, / some wrapped in rough cloth . . . their coverings / coming loose" so the corpses lose any semblance of a dignified death; "The Dead" is actually a revision of an uncollected poem Olds published in 1979 titled "Leningrad Cemetery, 1914." In "When He Came for the Family" (11), the pointlessness of tyranny is symbolized by a child's cello, smashed by an unidentified marauder. Other themes in "War" include murderous psychosis ("The Smile," 15), victimization and profiteering ("Free Shoes," 16), practical bravery in the face of death ("The Body-Sniffers," 17), and selfless but self-obliterating heroism ("His Crew," 18). Olds reasserts her perennial idea of empathy and peace. Overall, however, the poems in "War" are more perfunctory than earlier sequences on the same subject. Olds's language is terse to the point of recitation and lacks her usual power. Part of this may be the nature of outreach. Protest poetry, to reach as many readers as possible, must be accessible, and "War" follows an aesthetic that makes for easy reading. One could label these poems as naturalist (concerned with the effect of environment on characters) or imagist (presenting the poetic subject without sentimental embellishment), and Olds's distillation of images unfolds with this level of sophistication, even if the presentation is somewhat flat.

Three in "War" do deserve closer analysis, considered here in reverse order to make a point. In "The Body" (19) Olds imagines a soldier with "pieces of plastic and steel in it" (the pronoun suggesting dehumanization), trying to move and feel after the detonation of a bomb or landmine. The language is highly lyrical as Olds describes the lost animating spirit of the soldier's body, "the lovely one is gone, the one who / rode it, rider on a mount, the one who had / a name and spoke." This is Olds at her most sorrowful. While meaning in the poem is limited to antiwar protest, the poem is one of her most emotional; the emotive power of personalizing the dead body comes from the reminder that life is vulnerable and beautiful. "The Body" is the closing statement of the sequence and sums up her overarching somatic theme, which includes sex, procreation, and parenting: once again echoing Whitman, Olds asserts that biology needs spirit.

She reserves her ire for "The Leader" (13). The subject is a male warmonger, representing the politico, dictator, king, general, or president who seeks glory from the blood of others while himself dying of old age. Olds imagines statues of the leader "in every capital city of his nation / around the world" to make clear that this is not any particular monster but a repeating human phenomenon. He is falsely a "Friend to the Children." One is reminded of any number of modern dictators (from Adolf Hitler to Saddam Hussein) who used their young citizens, endangered by jingoism and warfare, as public relations props. Always Olds asserts the importance of protecting the future.

But the strongest statement comes in the middle of the section: "The Signal" (12). The poem tells the story of a war hero's storming a beachhead in an invasion very much like D-Day. He lands to find his force's "tanks burning, / the guns thrown down." Donning white gloves, he turns his back to his enemies and motions the other landing craft to retreat. When he is killed, his wife—safely in the domestic sphere—is given his medal. Through a "wall of smoke," she sees him in her dreams. In the dream he is facing her, "the gloves blazing on his hands as he motioned her back." The war hero tells his wife, *No. Go back, do not follow. Retreat to life.* This is Olds's message overall, to her readers, to anyone who will listen, but most especially to the women in her audience.

NOTES

Chapter 1—Understanding Sharon Olds

1. Halladay, "Sharon Olds," 2489.

2. Ibid.

3. Tennessee Williams, scene 1 production notes in *The Glass Menagerie* (New York: New Directions, 1999), 3.

4. Logan, "No Mercy," 29.

5. Kirsch, "Sharon Olds," 273.

6. Wright, review of *The Dead and the Living*, 151.

7. Hoagland, "Unarrestable Development," 8.

8. See Delmore Schwartz, "In Dreams Beging Responsibilities," in *In Dreams Begin Responsibilities and Other Stories* (New York: New Directions, 1978), 1–9.

9. Diane Wood Middlebrook and Diana Hume George, eds., *Selected Poems of Ann Sexton* (Boston: Houghton Mifflin, 2000), iv.

10. Shivani, "American Poetry in an Age of Constriction, " 205.

11. Hempel, "Sharon Olds," 27.

Chapter 2—Manifestos

1. Durrant, "Sharon Olds."

2. Lewellan, "Signature Poetics," 33.

3. Estess, review of *Satan Says*, 92.

4. From an interview at the New York State Writer's Institute's afternoon seminar, January 29, 1998, available at the Modern American Poetry website, http://www.english.illinois.edu/maps/poets/m_r/olds/onlineinterviews.htm.

5. Kirsch, "Sharon Olds," 272.

6. Ibid.

7. Tucker, "Family Ties," 14.

8. Quoted in Patterson, "Sharon Olds."

9. Dino Felluga, "Modules on Lacan. II: The Structure of the Psyche," http://www.cla.purdue.edu/english/theory/psychoanalysis/lacanstructure.html (accessed October 31, 2015).

10. Graham and Sontag, "Introduction: Containing Multitudes," 3.

11. Lea, "Making a Case," 39.

12. Joan Aleshire, 16.

13. Judith Harris, 259.

14. Collins, "My Grandfather's Tackle Box," 84.
15. Ibid., 90.
16. Ibid., 90.

Chapter 3—The Father Poems

1. See Mulvey, *Visual and Other Pleasures,* 14–29.
2. Plath, Sylvia. "Sylvia Plath and Ted Hughes Talk about Their Relationship," BBC radio interview, British Library Sound Archive, 1961, http://www.theguardian.com/books/audio/2010/apr/15/sylvia-plath-ted-hughes (accessed January 5, 2016). See also Jill Scott, *Electra after Freud: Myth and Culture* (Ithaca, N.Y.: Cornell University Press, 2005).
3. Scheponik, "Olds's 'My Father Speaks,'" 59.
4. Ibid., 60.

Chapter 4—The Mother Poems

1. See McAuliffe's biographical information on the NASA website, http://www.jsc.nasa.gov/Bios/htmlbios/mcauliffe.html (accessed October 31, 2015).
2. Burnside, para. 1. See also: http://www.thenation.com/article/readers-respond-sharon-olds/

Chapter 5—Love, Good Sex, Bad Sex, Sex and Marriage, Divorce

1. Sylvia Plath, "Bucolics," in *The Collected Poems,* edited by Ted Hughes (San Francisco: Harper & Row, 1981), 23.
2. Anne Sexton, "Old Dwarf Heart," in *All My Pretty Ones* (Boston: Houghton Mifflin, 1962), 10.
3. Pride, "Interview with Sharon Olds."

Chapter 6—War, Suicide, Freaks

1. Gunne and Thompson, "Introduction: Feminism without Borders."
2. See Laddie Lucas, *Flying Colours: The Epic Story of Douglas Bader* (London: Hutchinson, 1981).

BIBLIOGRAPHY

Works by Sharon Olds

Blood, Tin, Straw. New York: Knopf, 2001.

"Bop after Hip Op," *New Yorker,* August 11, 2014.

The Dead and the Living. New York: Knopf, 1984.

"Douche-Bag Ode." *Ploughshares* 39 (Spring 2013): 104.

The Father. New York: Knopf, 1997.

Foreword to *What Silence Equals,* by Tory Dent. New York: Persea Books, 1993.

The Gold Cell. New York: Knopf, 2001.

"Leningrad Cemetery, Winter of 1941." *New Yorker,* December 31, 1979, 51.

"Meeting a Stranger." *Ploughshares* 39 (Spring 2013): 105–6.

One Secret Thing. New York: Knopf, 2008.

"Open Letter to Laura Bush." *Nation*, October 10, 2005.

Preface to *The Orgy: An Irish Journey of Passion and Transformation,* by Muriel Rukeyser. Ashfield, Mass.: Paris, 1997.

"Return to Key West after My Mother's Death." *Southern Review* 47 (Autumn 2011): 533.

Satan Says. Pittsburgh: University of Pittsburgh Press, 1980.

"Sixteen Poems: A Special APZ Supplement. What Left?" *American Poetry Review* 40 (November–December 2011). 30–36.

Stag's Leap. New York: Knopf, 2012.

Strike Sparks: Selected Poems, 1980–2002. New York: Knopf, 2004.

The Unswept Room. New York: Knopf, 2001.

"Vogue Shoot." In "True Original: Pulitzer Prize Winner Sharon Olds Shares a Poem about Being Photographed for *Vogue*." *Vogue,* September 2012. http://www.vogue.com/873114/true-original-pulitzer-prize-winner-sharon-olds-writes-a-new-poem-about-being-photographed-for-vogue/.

The Wellspring. New York: Knopf, 1995.

Interviews

Blossom, Laurel. "Interview with Sharon Olds." *Poets and Writers* September/October 1993, 30–37.

Durrant, Sabine. "Sharon Olds: Confessions of a Divorce." *Guardian,* January 26, 2013. http://www.theguardian.com/lifeandstyle/2013/jan/26/sharon-olds-american-poet-divorce.

Garner, Dwight. "The Salon Interview: Sharon Olds." *Salon,* July 1, 1996. http://www.salon.com/1996/07/01/interview_19/.

Haskell, Arlo. "Sharon Olds: 2003." KWLS Audio Archives, the Beautiful Changes. Audio blog post, April 4, 2008. http://www.kwls.org/podcasts/sharon_olds_2003/.

Hempel, Amy. "Sharon Olds." *Bomb* 54 (Winter 1996): 24–27.

Laskey, Michael. "Advice to Young Poets: Sharon Olds in Conversation." Poets.org. http://www.poets.org/poetsorg/text/advice-young-poets-sharon-olds-conversation (accessed November 14, 2015).

Macdonald, Marianne. "Olds's Worlds." *Guardian* July 25, 2008. http://www.theguardian.com/books/2008/jul/26/poetry.

Patterson, Christina. "Sharon Olds: Blood, Sweat, and Fears." *Independent* October 27, 2006. http://www.independent.co.uk/arts-entertainment/books/features/sharon-olds-blood-sweat-and-fears-421691.html.

Pride, Mike. "Interview with Sharon Olds, Pittsfield's Pulitzer-prize winning poet." *Concord Monitor,* April 15, 2013. http://www.concordmonitor.com/doseetaste/5704786–95/an-interview-with-sharon-olds-pittsfields-pulitzer-winning-poet.

Schweig, Sarah V. "A Social Art." *Bomb,* September 5, 2012. http://bombmagazine.org/article/6809/.

Secondary References

Aleshire, Joan. "Staying News: A Defense of the Lyric." *After Confession*. St. Paul: Graywolf, 2001. 14–37.

Aube, Cory Michelle. "Through the Waves: Images of the Self in the Confessional Poetry of Sylvia Plath, Anne Sexton, Sharon Olds, and Kim Addonizio." M.A. thesis. Emporia State University, 2010.

Burnside, John. "A Different Kind of Truth." *Guardian*. September 27, 2006. http://www.theguardian.com/commentisfree/2006/sep/28/comment.bookscomment

Carlson, Celia. "Lyric Image as Sensuous Thought." *Journal of Modern Literature* 35.3 (Spring 2012): 158–82.

Collins, Billy. "My Grandfather's Tackle Box: The Limitations of Memory-Driven Poetry." In *After Confession: Poetry as Autobiography,* edited by Kate Sontag and David Graham, 81–91. Saint Paul, Minn.: Graywolf, 2001.

De Silva, Martha. "Strategies of Organization in Sharon Olds's 'Satan Says' and Senses of Loss." M.A. thesis. Georgetown University, 1989.

Dillon, Brian. "'Never Having Had You, I Cannot Let You Go': Sharon Olds's Poems of a Father-Daughter Relationship." *Literary Review* 37 (Fall 1993): 108–18.

Doty, Mark. "Secrets of the Flesh: Tender, Unsparing Poems on the Art of Forgiving." Review of *One Secret Thing. Oprah,* October 2008: 228.

Estess, Sybil P. Review of *Satan Says. Southern Humanities Review* 17, no. 1 (1983): 92–93.

Feaver, Vicki. "Body and Soul: The Power of Sharon Olds." In *Contemporary Women's Poetry: Reading/Writing/Practice,* edited by Alison Mark and Deryn Rees-Jones, 140–56. New York: Palgrave, 2000.

Flint, Roland. "A Way of Knowing." *Poet Lore* 83 (Spring 1988): 39–44.

Gill, Jo, ed. *Modern Confessional Writing: New Critical Essays.* London: Routledge, 2006.

Gore, Melissa-Leigh. "Love Invents the Body That Is Not an Object: Feminist Body Poetics in Sharon Olds." M.A. thesis, Brandies University, 2013.

Graham, David, and Kate Sontag. "Introduction: Containing Multitudes." In *After*

Confession: Poetry as Autobiography, edited by Kate Sontag and David Graham, 3–9. Saint Paul, Minn.: Graywolf, 2001.

Gunne, Sorcha, and Zoë Brigley Thompson. "Introduction: Feminism without Borders: The Potentials and Pitfalls of Retheorizing Rape." In *Feminism, Literature and Rape Narratives: Violence and Violation,* edited by Sorcha Gunne and Zoë Brigley Thompson, 1–21. London: Routledge, 2009.

Hamilton, Ian, ed. "Sharon Olds. In *The Oxford Companion to Twentieth-Century Poetry in English*. Oxford: Oxford University Press, 1994. 398.

Harris, Judith. "Breaking the Code of Silence: Ideology and Women's Confessional Poetry." In *After Confession*. St. Paul: Graywolf, 2001. 254–268.

Hoagland, Tony. "The Unarrestable Development of Sharon Olds." *American Poetry Review* 38 (January/February 2009): 7–9.

Holden, Jonathan. "Sharon Olds." *American Poetry: 1970–1990. A Profile of Twentieth-Century American Poetry,* edited by Josh Myers and David Abjohn, 254–74. Carbondale: Southern Illinois University Press, 1991.

Holladay, Hilary. "Sharon Olds." In *Critical Survey of Poetry.* English language edition, vol. 5, edited by Frank Magill. Pasadena: Salem Press, 1992. 2489–2494.

Kirsch, Adam. "Sharon Olds." In *The Modern Element: Essays on Contemporary Poetry,* 271–79. Norton: New York. 2008.

Lea, Sydney. "Making a Case; or, 'Where Are You Coming From?'" In *After Confession: Poetry as Autobiography,* edited by Kate Sontag and David Graham, 38–50. Saint Paul, Minn.: Graywolf, 2001.

Leahy, Anna. "Is Women's Poetry Passé? A Call for Conversation." *Legacy* 25, no. 2 (2008): 311–23.

Lewellan, Walter E. "The Signature Poetics of Sharon Olds and John Cage." Ph.D. diss., University of South Florida, 2006.

Logan, William. "No Mercy." Review of *Blood, Tin, Straw. New Criterion* 18 (December 1999): 29.

Matson, Suzanne. "Talking to Our Father: The Political and Mythical Appropriations of Adrienne Rich and Sharon Olds." *American Poetry Review* 18 (November/December 1989): 35–41.

McDiarmid, Lucy. "Private Parts." *New York Times Book Review,* May 15, 1996, 15.

"Modern American Poetry: Sharon Olds." *Modern American Poetry.* University of Illinois at Urbana-Champaign. http://www.english.illinois.edu/maps/poets/m_r/olds/olds.htm.

Monoghan, Patricia. "'She Want It All': The Sun Goddess in Contemporary Women's Poetry." *Frontiers: A Journal of Women's Studies* 11 (1990): 21–25.

Montefiore, Janet. "The Doctoral Defense." Review of *Blood, Tin, Straw. Times Literary Supplement,* March 2, 2001, 24.

Mulvey, Laura. *Visual and Other Pleasures.* New York: Palgrave Macmillan, 2009.

Ostriker, Alicia. "I Am (Not) This: Erotic Discourse in Bishop, Olds, and Stevens." *Wallace Stevens Journal* 19 (Fall 1995): 234–54. Reprinted in *Dancing at the Devil's Party: Essays on Poetry, Politics, and the Erotic.* Ann Arbor: University of Michigan Press, 2003.

———. "The Tune of Crisis." *Poetry* 149 (January 1987): 231–37.

Scheponik, Peter C. "Olds's 'My Father Speaks to Me from the Dead.'" *Explicator* 57 (1998): 59–62.

Schultz, Susan M. "The Double Burden of American Poets." *Virginia Quarterly Review* 65 (1989): 773–84.

Shivani, Anis. "American Poetry in an Age of Constriction." *Cambridge Quarterly* 35, no. 3 (2006): 206–30.

"Sharon Olds." In *Contemporary Literary Criticism,* vol. 32. Detroit: Gale, 1985. 345–47.

"Sharon Olds: State Poet 1998–2000." November 28, 2000. http://www.albany.edu/writers-inst/webpages4/archives/olds.html. Siemon, Cordula. *The Depiction of Human Misery in Sharon Olds's "The Food-Thief" and Adrienne Rich's "Shattered Head."* Munich: GRIN, 2013.

Smith, Aaron. "The Very Act of Telling: Sharon Olds and Writing Narrative Poetry." Poets.org, January 4, 2005. http://www.poets.org/poetsorg/text/very-act-telling-sharon-olds-and-writing-narrative-poetry.

Smith, Dinitia. "The Creative Mind: The Examined Life, without Punctuation." *New York Times,* September 9, 1999. http://www.nytimes.com/1999/09/09/books/the-creative-mind-the-examined-life-without-punctuation.html.

Sutton, Brian. "Olds's 'Sex without Love.'" *Explicator* 55, no. 3 (1997): 177–80.

Swiontkwoski, Gale. *Imagining Incest: Sexton, Plath, Rich and Olds on Life with Daddy.* Selinsgrove, Penn.: Susquehanna University Press, 2003.

Tanner, Laura E. "Death-Watch: Terminal Illness and the Gaze in Sharon Olds's *The Father.*" *Mosaic: A Journal for the Interdisciplinary Study of Literature* 29 (March 1996): 103–21.

Wineapple, Brenda. "I Have Done This Thing." Review of *Stike Sparks. Poetry* 185, no. 3 (2004): 232–36. http://www.poetryfoundation.org/poetrymagazine/browse/185/3#!/20606831.

Wakefield, Richard. "Olds's Poems Delve into Depths of Love." *Seattle Times,* January 16, 2000.

Tucker, Ken. "Family Ties." *New York Times Book Review,* March 18, 1984, 14.

Wright, Carolyne. Review *The Dead and the Living. Iowa Review* 15, no. 1 (1985): 151–61.

INDEX